A CHILD LEARNS
TO SPEAK

A CHILD LEARNS TO SPEAK

A Guide for Parents and Teachers of Preschool Children

By

Susan M. Leitch

Speech Pathology
University of Montana
Missoula, Montana

CHARLES C THOMAS ● PUBLISHER

Springfield ● Illinois ● U.S.A.

Published and Distributed Throughout the World by

CHARLES C THOMAS ● PUBLISHER

Bannerstone House

301-327 East Lawrence Avenue, Springfield, Illinois, U.S.A.

With THOMAS BOOKS *careful attention is given to all details of
manufacturing and design. It is the Publisher's desire to present books that
are satisfactory as to their physical qualities and artistic possibilities and
appropriate for their particular use.* THOMAS BOOKS *will be true to those
laws of quality that assure a good name and good will.*

Printed in the United States of America
R-2

Library of Congress Cataloging in Publication Data

Leitch, Susan M
  A child learns to speak.

  Bibliography: p.
  Includes index.
  1. Children--Language. 2. Child development.
I. Title.
LB1139.L3L39   372.6   76-24872
ISBN 0-398-03599-7

INTRODUCTION

WHEN your child says his* first words, he takes a major step toward successful communication. Speaking is perhaps one of the most important communication skills he will learn. Your child's ability to speak and use language will greatly affect his future success in life. We humans spend most of the time invested in our interactions with others in simply talking. This is our own unique ability. No other animals use such a complex symbol system for communication.

The task your child will undertake in learning to talk is quite complicated; speech and language themselves are complex processes. As an adult, you spend so much of your time speaking or listening that you take these skills for granted. However, talking involves the precise, coordinated movement of fifty to sixty muscles located in the mouth, face, neck, and abdomen, all directed by information stored in the brain.

Your child *learns* to speak. Although he also learns to walk and feed and dress himself, this task of learning to speak is a much more difficult job for him. Children learn to talk from those around them at home during the preschool years. Therefore, as a parent you are not a mere caretaker of physical needs, but truly a teacher. You teach your child, as we shall see, by being a good speech and language model. Your child learns from the examples you provide within your own speech. From the continuous flow of speech around him, your child determines what sounds are used to make up the words, what the words mean, and finally, how to join them together to express a thought. If you have ever listened to a foreign language, you have some notion of the confusion of sounds bombarding your child's ears as he begins to learn his language.

---

*The use of the masculine pronoun is used throughout the text to refer to children of both sexes for the sake of simplicity.

By the age of three and one-half to four years, your child no longer sounds as if he is using "baby-talk." Some of his utterances, for the first time, are complete and well formed. Even though he has much to learn, his speech begins to resemble yours by this age. How is it that children accomplish such a complicated feat so early in life? What are the processes at work that allow early language acquisition in your child? What should you expect of your child at various stages of language learning and what can you do as parent and teacher to assist the process? What type of environment at home is best for learning language and speech?

This guide is designed to help you the parent to answer these and other questions about your child's speech and language development. It includes some of the most current knowledge developed from the research of the 1960's and early 1970's. Language and speech are learned in the home with parents as the primary teachers; therefore, by understanding the normal course of speech and language development, you can aid your child in ways that help rather than hinder. It is hoped that this guide will answer some of your major questions and suggest what you can do to assist your child. In addition, checkpoints in normal speech and language development are provided, so that you may follow his progress.

The guide is organized into eight chapters and includes a glossary at the end of the text. The first chapter describes a good language-learning home environment. The remaining chapters are divided into seven discussions of speech and language development covering the ages from birth to six months, six to twelve months, twelve to eighteen months, eighteen to twenty-four months, two to three years, three to four years, and four to five years. The stages of development are divided by age for convenience and clarity in presentation and do not necessarily denote clear-cut stages of language development. You do need to read the guide from the beginning, since many of the processes described at one age division will continue into the next age division.

Each chapter, excluding the first, is organized for your convenience as follows. The first topic is language development, and speech development is the second major topic of interest. These two topics are succeeded by a section entitled "Parental Guidelines" which is intended to help you to be a good speech and language teacher. Since the development of speech and language skills in your child closely parallels his development of physical (motor) skills, a brief description of the child's physical skills is provided for each age division. The final entry in each chapter is a list of checkpoints. These are lists of skills which your child accomplishes during the respective age periods with respect to language, speech, and physical development.

The purpose of the checkpoints is twofold. First, they summarize the typical accomplishments of your child during the different stages of development. This is helpful in determining what expectations you should have for your child's speech and language skills at different ages. Second, the checkpoints can warn you that a child may be having difficulties.

Most children learn to talk in similar ways with a similar sequence of development. That is, they proceed from the simple to the complex skills in speech and language. There is, however, much variability from child to child in the age at which he attains a particular skill as well as the time it takes to perfect that skill. In the discussions of development relating to age, the age given is an average figure representing a wide range of possible ages considered to be normal. Any book about children must overgeneralize and can never be so comprehensive as to portray completely an individual child. Instead, we refer to the mythical child of average weight, average height, and average language ability.

ACKNOWLEDGMENTS

T HE author wishes to express sincere appreciation to the following people for their assistance in the preparation of this book: Dr. Evan Jordan, Ms. Barbara Bain, and Ms. Joan Christopherson of the University of Montana, who reviewed this work. Special thanks is due my husband, William Leitch, who spent many hours proofing and typing the material.

S.M.L.

CONTENTS

A CHILD LEARNS
TO SPEAK

1

SPEECH, LANGUAGE, AND
THE CHILD'S ENVIRONMENT

Definitions of Speech and Language

The definitions of speech and language are important.

WHAT do we mean when we use the words *speech* and *language*, and how are these affected by your child's environment? *Speech* refers to the actual production of the sounds making up words. These sounds are produced by the coordination of muscles and the flow of air through the larynx (voice-box). *Language* refers to our complex system of symbols used to communicate. We use it to refer to things around us, to express relationships, feelings, thoughts, and to convey messages to others in written or oral form. When we want to communicate with others, we use our system of symbols — language — to form the message so others understand it. Language includes words and their meanings, word order, the rules that govern word combinations, and the speech sounds that compose the words. Communication, then, involves both speech and language. Speech is our language used orally.

We often divide language into two types: *expressive* and *receptive*. *Expressive* language is that which we ourselves compose; it is what we say to others. *Receptive* language is that which we hear and must interpret; someone else has produced it. Receptive language skills enable us to understand the language spoken around us. Your child must acquire skill in both language types. You may notice that your child understands more words or sentences than he can say. This is usually the case, and is normal, since a child must first learn to understand a fragment of language before he can say it. The development during the preschool years of both receptive and expressive language skills is discussed in the following chapters.

3

The Innate Capacity for Language

Your child has an innate capacity for language.

It is believed that man is born with the ability to learn language. What does this mean to the parent? It means that your child has a built-in capacity to perceive and learn the language of his environment whatever it may be — English, French, or Navajo. There are certain aspects of language that the child does not have to learn, but will bring with him to the task of learning language. For example, the infant is particularly sensitive to speech sounds. It appears that he is biologically programmed to be able to hear speech. He also has the ability to imitate the speech sounds he hears around him. These sounds have a function, and he acts as if he understands this and begins to learn this function. Something in the composition of his brain, which is unlike or absent from other animal brains, allows him to learn language. The chimpanzee, for example, is a relatively intelligent animal, and easily trained. However, even with intensive language training, it is unable to develop the rudiments of spoken language. Language is acquired by humans over a wide range of intellectual ability. Your child's acquisition of language, unless he is severely retarded, is most responsive to a good home environment. The human species has an inborn capacity to learn language. It is this innate ability which allows the child to learn language so early in life.

Even so, the desire to learn language must be triggered and sustained by the child's environment. This means that if he were to grow up on an island, isolated from other humans, he would not develop language. Your child will learn from you. You provide the language examples that he will learn to decipher and eventually say himself. Remember you are his speech and language model.

The Need for Nonlinguistic Experience

A good home environment and nonverbal communication are important for your child.

The environment you provide for your child in the home and

the interaction between you and him are important, and affect the quality of his speech and language development. The heart of successful communication is the close, tender relationship between you and your child from his birth. That is, great importance is placed on the social context in which language is learned. You and your child begin the process of communicating in nonverbal ways: Your first interactions involve those of touching and caressing; a closeness and warmth from one another's bodies communicates love and care to the infant. He gains a sense of security from your touch, warmth, smell, tone of voice, and facial expression. Gradually, as the infant grows older, seeing and hearing become more important than the touching and smelling in the communication act. You coo, play, and use facial gestures to express your joy and pleasure with one another. Eventually, you will share words. It is by this pleasurable early nonverbal communication, as well as by talking, that the child is motivated to learn even more and better ways to communicate with you.

Your child gives information to you by crying and later by gestures. He extends his arms to indicate that he wants "up." He wiggles to show excitement. His crying tells you that he wants something done about his predicament. Facial expressions — smiling and frowning — communicate very definitely how he feels about matters. You smile and he returns your smile. Indeed, much communication takes place before the first words.

Studies show us that those children whose early attempts at communication are unanswered develop speech and language at a slower rate. A child who is frequently left crying in his crib experiences failure with this most basic form of communication. Successive failures in communication attempts only seem to prove to the child that there is no reason to continue his efforts; the environment does not satisfy his needs for love, care, and attention. He may then perceive the environment as hostile, and his attempts to communicate with it will diminish.

It is obvious that the more interaction that you have with your child showing concern and consideration, the more likely he is to want to continue to communicate with you. These interactions also increase the opportunity for you to provide a language model. It is believed that the pleasant feeling involved in early nonspeech communication between the parent and child provides the motivating force for the child to want to develop speech. He has a reason and a need for communicating, and most importantly, he has you to communicate with. Babies brought up in child-care institutions are generally delayed in language acquisition precisely because they do not have this early, frequent, and loving human contact.

A Good Language-Learning Environment

Your child needs to explore his environment.

Your child not only needs and learns from many examples of language, but he needs to learn about his world in general. He needs what we call nonlinguistic experience (discovering and playing with objects and events around him) as well as linguistic experience (exposure to talking). Your child develops an understanding of the nature of things around him before he develops language. At first, he learns about the world through his body. He perceives what surrounds him by looking at it, touching it, feeling it, listening to it, smelling it, tasting it, and moving about within it. He forms concepts about his world based on what he is able to understand about it. He will, for example, form the concepts of hot and cold by touching, loud and soft by listening, near and far by crawling and walking, big and little by looking. From his explorations your child organizes and orders what he sees into spatial patterns; he learns that the door is over there, the table here, and the ceiling up there. He will notice different shapes and sizes as he begins to analyze his world. He also develops an understanding of distances and of three dimensions, and thus can determine the relationships of objects to each other. Similarly, he patterns sensations through the other senses of hearing, touching, smelling, and tasting. To do these things the child must have the freedom to explore, investigate, and play with things. He will learn very little while flat on his back in a crib or playpen. Your child may "get into things" around the house during this period, but he is gaining valuable information, and is storing it away.

These concepts, which form the basis for the understanding of his environment, may seem rather obvious to you as an adult, but your child must learn them. For example, he must learn that objects have permanence. They do not disappear into thin air just because he can no longer see them. If a ball is put first under a cup and then put under a handkerchief, the child must learn to look for it under the handkerchief and not the cup. He learns to order a sequence of events.

These are but a few examples of the nonlinguistic experiences that are necessary for concept formation which in turn is necessary to normal language development. Your child increases his knowledge of the world through his various activities and explorations and you can make these rich and plentiful for him.

You can provide a good environment for language learning for your child.

You are the speech and language model in the child's environment. You can change your speech in ways that help him to learn language. You can do this by repeating words or phrases, pointing or using other gestures when you are talking, exaggerating your speech, and speaking more slowly. Parents may naturally use simplified, shorter, more redundant sentences when talking to their children. All of these things are helpful cues to language for your child.

A noisy environment increases the difficulty of the language-learning task. It is harder for your child to pick out the fleeting speech sounds in words. There may be so many sounds bombarding the child that he could be unable to make sense out of any of them. If so, he will have trouble in language learning. Your child benefits from time you set aside for talking and playing with him, time free from other distracting noises or activities.

The amount of time spent fondling and talking to your child affects the rate of language development. The more interaction you have with your child — just the two of you — the better. It is important to the language-learning process. As a result of such attention, first born and only children usually begin to talk sooner than children of the same age with brothers and sisters. The first born usually get more individual attention from the parents, because time does not have to be divided up among other youngsters. Even if you have a house-full of children, set aside some time to be alone with your language-learning children, especially during their preschool years.

Your home environment needs to provide the child with a loving relationship, personal interactions, satisfaction in communication, language examples, and nonlinguistic experiences. From these your child organizes his world and his language until it matches that of the adults around him. Let us now follow this process from birth on.

2

BIRTH TO SIX MONTHS
HUNGER CRIES AND COMFORT COOS

MOST parents, when asked when their child first began to talk, will respond, "Oh, he was about a year old." Although his first words are said then, the child has gone through many preparatory speech-learning exercises before he has achieved his first words. Speech begins with the birth cry. Let us see why and how.

Language Development

At this stage your child is not using language in the strict sense of the word. We can not yet analyze his words, word order, or word meanings. We can, however, look at some events that form the foundations for the future development of language.

Your child develops his listening skills.

To acquire language your child must be able to hear. Listening skills are the receptive beginnings of language. His ability to listen will improve as he develops and matures.

The infant's first response to sound is observed as an increase or decrease of movement all over his body immediately following the sound. In the earliest stages the sound must be loud to produce such response in the infant. Closer observation following the presentation of a loud sound may reveal a quick closing of the eyes (or tightening of the eyelids if they are already closed). As the infant matures, another early response to sound is that of "staring." After the presentation of the sound the infant's eyes are fixed as if he is staring at something. At about three months of age the infant begins to search for the source of the sound by turning his head and eyes toward its source. This response is well developed by six months of age. The infant proceeds from gross, undifferentiated responses to sound to fine, more specific responses as his system matures. It should be noted that the responses described above can be produced by touching the infant or by a change in his visual field. Therefore, when observing his response to sound he should not be touched or distracted visually.

The infant's reaction to speech sounds also goes through a series of changes. In the first week of life the infant may stop whimpering when he hears a soft voice. He may stare, smile, or stop crying in response to a human voice by two or three months of age. Around four months of age the infant can tell the difference between angry and friendly voices, as well as familiar and unfamiliar voices. If the responses outlined above are missing from an infant's behavior when he hears a sound, it could be due to a hearing impairment. If there is some doubt, his hearing should be checked by an audiologist. There exist today techniques to test the hearing of a child of any age.

As you talk to your child at this stage, your tone of voice reveals more than anything else what you are saying to him. In fact, he recognizes pitch patterns in your voice before he recognizes the words. For example, he understands the way you say, "Good night," not by the words, but by your tone of voice. You could use any two similar words with the same tone of voice and he would think it meant, "Good night." Since he does not yet understand words, he relies more on some of your common gestures.

Crying is your child's language now.

The first howling of your infant is undifferentiated, no matter what the problem. The vocalizations he makes during his first two months are largely cries and other reflexive sounds made while eating, sucking, and swallowing. Then, gradually, you will be able to hear a difference between the cries of hunger, discomfort, and pain; your child is communicating his first information to the world he has entered. He learns very early how persuasive his crying is in bringing you rushing in to serve his needs. He has learned the importance of communicating and finds it rewarding, so that his motives for learning language have been strengthened.

Speech Development

Even your child's crying is important to the learning process.

Crying is important, as he is learning to feel the flow of air through his larynx, nose, and mouth. He is also developing a unique breathing pattern in his crying, the same pattern that is essential for speech. Breath patterns for speech differ from those used in simply breathing. Your child will perhaps, much to your dismay, cry very loudly or perhaps at a very high pitch. He must learn the breath patterns for speech, as well as the control of the pitch and loudness of his voice.

New muscles affecting his vocalizations are being discovered all the time by the infant. He learns what muscles make changes in loudness and pitch. Changes in the shape of your child's mouth also allow him to make more and varied sounds. Growth processes move his tongue downward and back in his mouth and the roof of his mouth moves downward. These changes give him more tongue flexibility. Then sounds such as vowels and consonants can be more readily made.

What is the nature of the sounds your child makes?

Your child learns from his crying, as pointed out above, but certainly not from crying all the time. More speech sounds are practiced during states of contentment. During his sighs, grunts, and gurgles, you may hear many sounds. He is beginning to put together his alphabet.

During the first couple of months, your child devotes a large part of his vocal effort to crying. He also makes many reflexive sounds following feeding that result from continued swallowing and sucking movements. Most of the sounds are vowel like. One vowel is uttered at a time, and they are not often repeated. The vowels, such as *uh, eh,* and *ih* predominate in his speech.

A new type of sound making becomes more evident at about three to four months of age. Your child begins to "babble." That is, he starts playing with sequences of sounds and syllables for his own pleasure. Some children babble often and others do not. Your child makes rhythmic coos from strings of sounds. In this sound play he mimics pitch patterns from your talking. He experiments with pitch and voice quality, both of which are necessary skills for speech. You may hear his babbling accompanied by screeching, screaming, laughing, or squealing. He may use a shrill, high pitch for anger and a low, full pitch for play.

Specific sound combinations are now evident in his sound making. At this stage he makes sound combinations and sequences from different vowels. These vowel patterns begin to decrease as syllable patterns with consonants appear, such as *ku-ga* or *he-haw*. Vowel sounds are easier for the child to make and are learned first. This is because they do not require the precise muscle movements and mouth positions that consonants require. He is learning a variety of sounds, and the sequences he makes will increase in length.

At this time you and your baby may have "cooing conversations." He coos to you and you return vocalization with an imitation of his coos. He listens and then wiggles with excitement as he coos back to you in return. You imitate your child's sound making now, but in the next six months he will be imitating your sound making.

In his babbling, your child produces more and more of the speech sounds he hears in his environment. You may distinguish the following consonants in his speech: *k, g, h, d, w, m,* and *b*. However, he makes most frequent use of the *k, h,* and the *g*. Sometimes you will hear your child practicing these sounds in private. He is learning to associate the sound he makes with the particular movements of his mouth. Allow your child this time to practice alone, but take the many other opportunities to stimulate your baby with your speech.

How does your child learn to make speech sounds?

Your child learns to make the sounds he hears in *your* speech. He does not, for example, begin to learn the sound system of the family dog or cat. He has the ability, biologically, to discriminate or pick out speech sounds from all the other sounds in his environment, as well as an innate urge to make sounds and to select and imitate sounds around him. Even deaf babies have this innate urge to babble, but they soon quit for they obtain no pleasure from hearing the sounds.

You play a large role in the child's acquisition of speech sounds. Children associate adult speech with the care, loving, and feeding provided for them. Thus, the speech itself brings forth favorable memories and feelings in the child. The child then enjoys imitating those speech sounds to which he has an emotional attachment. The child follows a progression of imitating more of the speech sounds around him until he approaches his first words. You motivate the child to acquire speech sounds by rewarding his sound making with smiles, caresses and pleasing tones of voice. Studies show that you can even affect the child's babbling in specific ways. For example, if you reward your child by smiling or caressing him every time he makes a consonant sound, his production of consonants in babbling will increase. Therefore, the verbal environment you surround the child with affects his verbal output.

Parental Guidelines

Stimulate your child with speech and with sound.

Talk to your child when you dress, feed, or bathe him. Keep it simple and consistent from one activity to another. You can play with him by imitating his gestures and sounds. In return he may imitate you. He will smile and vocalize to you during this stage. Babies need someone to "talk" to. Your child will be able to begin comprehending your gestures used with speech. Be consistent in the tone of voice and words used with the different gestures. This way your child can eventually learn the words. When you outstretch your arms to pick up the child, say "Up," for example. When you leave, wave and say, "Bye-bye." The tone of voice, the word, and the gesture become the rudiments of communication between you and your child.

Let your child hear as many different sounds as possible to help him develop his listening skills. Such things as chimes over his crib, a clock, soft music, or toys that make a noise will interest him and help him to associate certain sounds with certain objects.

Physical Development

The child has attained some physical as well as language milestones, so that by the time your child is babbling and practicing speech sounds, he can hold his head steadily in an erect position, sit up with props, and roll from his back to his stomach. As he matures physically, he will be able to coordinate his muscles to make more and varied utterances.

The following checkpoints, and all subsequent checkpoints, are based on average performance figures which represent a range of occurrence within plus or minus six months of the age indicated. If a delay in speech or language checkpoints extends over twelve months, a professional should be called in to determine the reason for the speech or language delay. There may be means by which to remedy the problem before it becomes more serious. It is significant that the child that matures more slowly should display slower development in both speech and language skills *and* physical skills. It is when these two patterns of development do not correlate well that there may be need for concern. If a child has poor language or speech but well-developed physical abilities, we may assume that the process of maturation is, in general, normal. Therefore, slower maturation in this case cannot be the cause of the language or speech delay. We then must ask the question, what *is* the cause of the delay? Slower maturation by itself is not necessarily cause for concern, but other causes for language or speech delay should at least be investigated.

Checkpoints

Your six-month-old child should be able to do the following:

Language and Speech Skills

(1) Respond vocally when socially stimulated.
(2) Respond to sounds by moving head and eyes toward the source of a sound.
(3) Coo, gurgle, and babble for pleasure and in private.

Physical Abilities

(1) Hold his head in an erect position.
(2) Sit up with props.
(3) Roll from back to stomach.
(4) Smile to caretakers.

SIX TO TWELVE MONTHS
GIBBERISH TO YOU, TOO

DURING this stage of development, your child's sound making becomes more complex and quite interesting. You probably hear him making endless sound patterns with definite rhythm and melody. A change also occurs in your child's babbling that is very noticeable. He seems to be giving you commands, asking questions, and making profound statements, all in his own truly unintelligible gibberish. Try as you may, you will not be able to understand him. This does not bother your child in the least. He continues to jabber to you, to others, and to his toys. He is approaching his first words, despite all the gibberish.

Language Development

Your child's expressive language skills at this stage are still minimal. He is just beginning to develop them. By the end of this period your child is close to finding and using his first meaningful words. We will consider these words in detail in Chapter 4. In this chapter, we will discuss the groundwork you and your child lay for those first words.

Your child builds up to his first word.

You may read a word into your child's babbling by accident. Among his many repetitions he may produce the syllable repetition, "Ma-ma." If you are present, you of course get excited, smile, and repeat back to your child what appears to you to be his first word. Your child now repeats the syllables *ma-ma* more often, not because he knows the word and who it stands for, but because it produces such favorable reactions from you.

He soon learns the word, though, because you repeat, "Mama," often to him now. It is through this type of exchange that words slowly begin to appear in his vocalizations. It is not easy to determine precisely when a child attaches meaning to the words he makes. To be sure, a word in his vocabulary emerges through a complex process over time. It does not happen instantly. Words are usually understood by your child before he says them, unless he is repeating them by accident, as in the example above.

Your child understands simple words, commands, and gestures.

While acquiring language, your child is able to comprehend more than he himself can say. That is, receptive language development precedes expressive language development. This is evidenced by the fact that although he does not say the words himself, he associates simple words you say to him with the appropriate activity or object. Such words as *mama, daddy, ball, dog, up, cookie, go,* and *bye-bye* may all be understood. Recall that your child first identified only the pitch patterns and inflections (tone of voice) in the words. Now he is able to recognize and understand the word itself. He responds to simple commands one at a time, such as "Come here," "Get down," "No-no," "Open your mouth," and "Find Mama." Your scolding and affectionate tones of voice have meaning for him at this age. Since he recognizes words, his pleasure and fascination in listening to you and others talk has increased.

Speech Development

Your child experiments with sound combinations.

The sounds, syllables, and sound patterns your child makes at this stage are longer and have more diversity than before. He has added many consonants to his repertoire, such as the *w, b, m, n, d,* and *t.* He is no longer relying so heavily on the *k, g,* and *h* for sound making. His vocalizations contain more of your speech sounds, and he is doing a better job of making them. You hear him form endless repetitions of the same sound patterns with rhythm and melody. He may say, "ba-ba-ba-ba," over and over again, or perhaps he varies the vowel to say, "me-ma-mu, me-ma-mu." He can repeat sounds and syllables in sequences because he has control over the sounds he makes. Nearly one third of his sound productions involve repeating consonant-vowel syllables, like *ba-ba-ba*. The number of sound and syllable repetitions contained in his utterances will increase until after his first birthday. Then they decrease through the entire developmental process. This repetitious nature of utterances is a *normal* stage in speech development. He not only experiments with different sound combinations, he plays with the pitches, loudness, and melodies of speech. These are all important skills in speaking.

Your child develops his own jargon.

Around eight months of age, the child's babbling changes. It becomes what we call jargon, a considerably more sophisticated form of babbling. Your child now has his own private jargon. His jargon appears to you to have meaning and purpose, but try as you will you probably cannot make any sense out of his gibberish. This unintelligible jabber sounds as if it contains questions, commands, and statements because he uses the proper inflection in his voice for these sentence types. He learns the inflectional patterns (melody and rhythm) of adult sentences long before he can make the sentences themselves.

He babbles quite frequently to you and others now, with definite and varied inflections in his voice. He seems to love displaying his new skills in speech. He also likes to imitate your gestures and perhaps some of your syllables or words. The words he imitates are usually one syllable or duplicate syllables such as *da-da, ma-ma, pa-pa,* or *bye-bye.* He picks out the accented syllable in a word and doubles it in his imitating to produce "da-da" for *daddy,* "ga-ga" for *all gone,* or "na-na" for *banana.* Your child answers back. Make a noise and he makes a noise. He enjoys imitating. If you are lucky, he waves "bye-bye" and even says it. His babbling, jargon, and interest in imitating will continue through the following period of language development. As he acquires more language skills, he has less use for his personal jargon and imitation. Do not forget that although most children proceed through the various stages of language development in a given order, activity in any one stage does not necessarily cease as soon as the next stage begins.

Parental Guidelines

You can help your child to acquire his first words more easily by using them consistently in the same situation and with an accompanying gesture if it is appropriate. Obvious examples of this are the use of "See the kitty" while pointing to the animal or extending your arms and saying "Want up?" Your child learns by hearing and seeing your words and gestures used over and over. He learns most easily that which you make obvious and simple for him. He learns his name, for example, if you say it often to him.

Your child benefits from both time talking alone and time talking with you and others. On his own he practices the sounds and syllables as he learns them. He uses this practice time to perfect his speaking ability.

At this age it is also helpful to your child if you associate the sounds with the objects that make them by pointing out the object as well as naming it. Such sounds as the telephone, the doorbell, or a dog barking provide good learning experiences. Your child should turn his head and shoulders toward the source of a sound, even if it is not loud and the object is not visible.

Your child needs the continued freedom to discover and explore his world, as mentioned in the first chapter. If necessary, the home should be "baby-proofed," so that he can investigate without causing trouble or hurting himself. Encourage him to play with objects that have a variety of colors, shapes, and textures. He is acquiring the nonlinguistic experience necessary for language acquisition.

Is your child's hearing impaired?

This is an important question to ask yourself at this time. If you have spent time gesturing and talking to your child, you have an idea of whether or not he is responding to your voice (not just your gestures). He begins imitating, producing, and understanding some simple language if he hears you. He uses his voice to get your attention. If this is not the case, ask yourself why. Could there be a hearing problem? Does he play with sounds and syllables in his jargon and respond to your voice and other noises around the home? If the answer is no, have your child's hearing checked immediately. Your public health nurse can direct you to your local speech and hearing service facilities.

If your child has a hearing impairment, he needs a great deal of extra instruction and training to learn language. Language and speech are learned primarily through the hearing mechanism, so if the child lacks the input of sound he lacks the basic information upon which language is built.

The hearing-impaired child must be discovered and helped as soon as possible! His impairment can be detected very early in life, and then he has the best chance to develop language despite his handicap. The early language-learning years, the first several years of life, can never be recaptured. That is, the child never finds it as easy to learn language as it is during these years. The reason for this is biological and related to his brain. It is thought that the child's mind is set in a predetermined way to process the structures of language with greatest ease during these critical years. A hearing-impaired child who does not receive early language training — before eighteen months of age — runs a risk of never developing to his full potential in language skills. Extra language training must be provided for the hearing-impaired child from babyhood on.

Physical Development

At this age your child is able to walk with support, grasp a toy and bring it to his mouth, stand alone, and drink from a glass with help. It is truly marvelous to see the progress he is making.

Checkpoints

Your twelve-month-old child should be able to do the following:

Language and Speech Skills

(1) Use his own jargon with inflection.
(2) Imitate sounds, simple words, or gestures.
(3) Respond to a simple command.
(4) Say one or duplicate-syllable words.
(5) Understand gestures and some words.
(6) Turn to the sound source even though its object is not visible.

Physical Abilities

(1) Walk with support.
(2) Grasp a toy or food and bring it to his mouth.
(3) Stand alone.
(4) Drink from a glass with help.

4

TWELVE TO EIGHTEEN MONTHS
FIRST WORDS, FIRST STEPS

THIS is an exciting stage for you. Your child is saying his first words and taking his first steps. He is not only standing on two instead of four legs, he is talking! His understanding of you is increasing all the time. He can follow simple commands and understand simple sentences. Your child still talks to those around him in his own personal jargon. He has fun imitating you. He acquires a few meaningful words by the end of the period, however, he will not combine these words until the next stage of language development. His talking is now limited to one-word utterances.

Language Development

Your child's first words carry a sentence's worth of meaning.

Your child's first talk consists of an abundance of his personal jargon as previously mentioned. However, as he acquires words with meaning, this behavior gradually decreases. He is developing his first expressive language skills with the use of his first words. The child's first words do not necessarily mean the same thing to him as they do to you. Your child does not yet combine words in his utterances; they are but one word in length. The one-word utterances may even be one-word puzzles. A whole sentence's worth of meaning is loaded into them. For example, "Milk!" may mean, "Give me some more milk!"; "Go" may mean, "Daddy has gone bye-bye." His earliest words are names or action words from things he does or sees. They may be words like *bye-bye, ball, no, mama, daddy, hi, mine, go, more,* or *cup.* Many of his words appear to you to have several meanings. This is because the child's first words have very broad meanings. While "Milk!" may mean a whole sentence, as pointed out above, it may stand for milk, snow, and vanilla ice cream as well. The categories of objects that fall under one word generally have one or two features in common. The child uses milk to refer to anything white and edible in the case above. The child may also create his own private word to stand for some of his broad categories. One child observed in a recent study used "peety" to stand for all brightly colored objects. Your child may build his word meanings on the basis of color, shape, size, function, movement, or some other readily observable characteristic. It is fun to try to determine what features your child is using in his word meanings by figuring out the common characteristics of the objects referred to by one word. It will take him time to acquire adult meanings.

At this stage his words appear only in one form and are not modified from that form. Your child does not yet add an *s* or other word ending to his newly acquired words. This is a very advanced skill which he will learn later.

Your child learns the name of an object.

Just how does your child learn to name an object? This is no simple matter, for in order to name an object, your child must have developed concepts about his world. He must be able to symbolize information in the form of speech sounds in a word. You have probably pointed out the object, a dog, to him many times while saying, "Doggie, this is a doggie." The child must decide at this point what it is that you are naming. That is, are you referring to the shape of the animal, its color, the way the animal moves, the animal itself, or the function of the animal, etc? Which one of these features, he wonders, means *dog*? He picks out a couple of features, such as shape and movement. A young child usually picks out the feature of shape first. So now your child calls everything on four legs that moves a "dog." He has overextended the use of the word and has not yet picked up all of the word's features. Later, as you point out cats, cows, and horses, he learns how to adjust his definitions of these animals to those of yours.

Children up to the age of two and one-half years overextend many of their new vocabulary words. Your child picks out the most obvious features of an object. Those features that are most outstanding to him depend upon his level of cognitive development, which is the degree to which he is able to perceive and organize information from the world around him. Some concepts are simply easier for him to comprehend. For example, he will learn to use the preposition *in* before he will use *under*. This is because he perceives an object as "in" before he is able to perceive it as "under" something. The same principle applies when he learns *long/short, hot/cold, big/little, more/less,* etc. He learns the first word of each of these pairs first. At this age, however, the second word in each pair means the same thing to him as the first word. This seems strange to us, of course, but your child is able to perceive positive aspects before he can perceive negative aspects. It is easy to say something is big (a positive aspect), but to say that something is little (a negative aspect) means that it lacks "bigness." To say that something is short is to say that it lacks "longness." But in order to know that it lacks "longness," he must know what long is. Therefore, he understands and learns to use the word *long* before the word *short*. Your child will acquire words only for those objects, situations, and relationships that he can perceive and understand, and which you name for him.

Your child's receptive language skills expand, too.

Your child probably recognizes the names of many common household objects. He can recognize an object in a picture when you name it. He can point to some parts of his body when you name them. As mentioned earlier, he understands your simple sentences, providing they are not too long. He can carry out commands like, "Put the ball on the table," "Give it to me," "Go get your shoes and socks," etc. Recall that his development of receptive language skills (comprehension of words and phrases) precedes his ability to say them himself. That which he only understands at this stage he will be producing in following stages of language development.

Speech Development

Give your child time to perfect his words

His first words often begin with the consonants *p, m, w, n, b, t,* or *d* because these are easier for him to pronounce. Your child is producing his first words and he is having trouble saying them correctly. He may say "baw" for *ball,* "daw" for *dog,* "wawah" for *water,* "poon" for *spoon,* "titta" for *sister.* Should you be worried? The answer is no. Your child may not completely perfect his ability to use speech sounds in words until the second grade in school. During this time the child is involved in the task of learning the adult sound system. You have specific rules and speech sounds in your sound system which he must learn through experience in listening and speaking. Through this experience he acquires various speech sounds and rules until his speech begins to more closely resemble yours.

Your child, in order to decipher your sound system, needs an ever increasing memory span as well as the ability to hear the difference between all the speech sounds. Then, in order to produce the sound he can hear and remember, he needs proper muscular control. As your child matures, so do the above skills necessary for learning and producing sounds. Therefore, as he grows older he is better able to produce more sounds. Some of our sounds are much harder to perceive and produce than others. These are usually the sounds that your child learns latest. Sounds such as *b* or *p* are easily seen on the lips and involve simpler movements than, say, the *s* or *ch* sounds, so they are more easily learned.

During his first year, your child has been making some sounds which are not in the English language. However, he is constantly increasing his production and practice of the speech sounds he hears spoken around him. It may be harder for him to produce a sound within a word than in babbling or jargon. At first, he produces many variations of a given sound when he uses it in a word. He may use both *tup* and *gup* for the word *cup.* Little by little, he will learn that *tup* and *gup* are not the same as *cup.* What appeared to your child to be varieties of the *kuh* sound drop out, and then he consistently uses that sound correctly in words. He understands the limits of the *kuh* sound. He can now properly produce and perceive that sound.

He must also learn to use the *c* in different positions in words. These positions are initial, medial, and final. A sound usually makes its first appearance in the initial position in a word, since it is learned most easily in that position. The sound may be used in the initial position for as long as a year before he uses it in the final or medial position. Before he completes the learning of a sound in all positions, you may hear him omit the sound and substitute another sound he already knows for a sound he has not learned. He may distort a newly learned sound when he is learning it, because he has not learned the boundaries of that sound. He is well on his way to learning the sound when he distorts it, rather than omitting it altogether or substituting another sound for it. Your child is constantly re-vising his sound system to match that of yours during his preschool years.

The sequence or order in which sounds are acquired by chil-dren is not consistent from child to child. However, most chil-dren will have learned some sounds by a certain age. These ages and sounds are illustrated in Table I, "The Acquisition of Speech Sounds." Generally, girls acquire sounds slightly faster than boys in our culture. Firstborn or only children will often acquire sounds sooner than other children. Consonant clusters are normally the last sounds that your child will learn to say. For example, he may say "poon" for *spoon* since the *sp* cluster is difficult for him. Such clusters as *str, bl, thr,* and *sw* are all difficult to say. Indeed, these are the last sounds he learns and adds to his sound system.

Your child has rhythm and melody in his speech.

The emphasis your child puts on the rhythm and repetition in his speech is striking. It appears to be an original and nat-ural style which is not imitated from an adult. Here is an

TABLE I

THE ACQUISITION OF SPEECH SOUNDS*

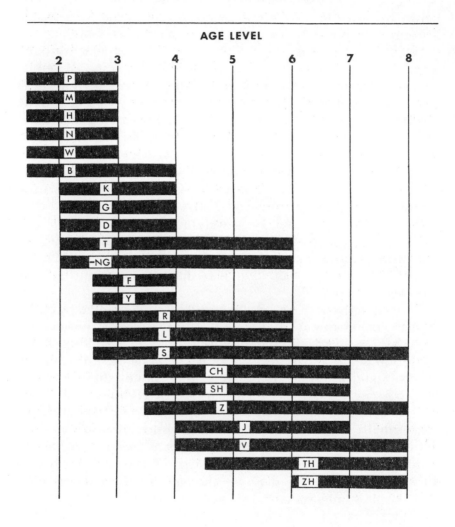

*The solid bar corresponding to each speech sound starts at the age at which 50% of all children pronounced it correctly; it stops at an age level at which 90% of all children pronounce the sound correctly. Those sounds that have a longer bar and which are acquired at a later age indicate a sound that is difficult to acquire. (Courtesy of E. Sanders, "When Are Speech Sounds Learned?" *Journal of Speech and Hearing Disorders, 37*:62, 1972.)

example from a child's running speech as he is looking at a book: "Book, book — buts buts buts tay tay gorsy, horsy. Horsy book, horsy book — yam yam yam yam horsy! horsy!" (Wyatt, 1969, p. 57). Notice the large number of repeated words that are said in almost a sing-song fashion. Many words at this age are repeated and the child seems to gain pleasure from these repetitions.

The melodies and inflections used by your child in his jargon are very adult like in some instances. This is why the utterances sound like many different sentences with meaning, but spoken in a foreign tongue. His jargon is loaded with many two-syllable nonsense words. At this age, he also loves to imitate your nonsense words as well as regular words.

Parental Guidelines

How best to help your child learn new words.

At this stage your child needs to hear words said over and over again in order to learn them. When you name an object or an action for him, use short, simple phrases. Do not drown the word in such a flood of language that he cannot pick it out. Use redundant sentences. "This is a *ball*. It is a *ball*. Catch the *ball!* Yes, it is Johnnie's *ball*. Throw the *ball!* All of these may be used in a running conversation to teach your child the word *ball*. Speak clearly, with slight emphasis on the word *ball*. When teaching a word, refrain from saying, "Say this" or Say that," but allow time for him to repeat it after you if he wishes. He will repeat the word when he is ready. Do not try to force it out of him. If he does not pronounce the word correctly, do not criticize his efforts, simply say the word again as a model for him to copy. In this way your child does not feel that he has said something wrong, and he is not made to feel badly about his first attempts. You cannot expect your child's speech to be perfect, since he is just getting started. His speech will need much refining through practice, as with any new skill that he learns. Once, however, you know that he can say a word and understands what the word means, encourage him to use the word. If he wants the ball, and only points to it, say "What? You tell me." If he makes an attempt, such as "baw," reward him for it by smiling and saying, "Good. Ball. Here is the ball." It is good practice to reward and praise your child for all of his speech attempts. This encourages him to continue to try to learn new forms.

Every time your child experiences a new object or feeling, supply him with a word for it. Your child is eager to investigate and learn about his world. Talk about what you are doing, such as cleaning, sewing, reading, building, washing, whatever it may be. Talk also about what your child is doing or what you are doing for him. For example, "We are going for a ride. Here is your coat. Let's put your coat on. Your coat is on." Talk to him about things he sees, hears, and does. Talk also about things that have happened recently and things that will happen in the near future, but do not forget to use short, concise sentences. This is not to imply that you talk to your child every minute of the day, but rather when there is a change of activity or a change in his state of being to explain.

Make your child feel like a part of the family by talking to him.

When speaking to your child, be consistent in the labels you give to objects or actions. In this way your language will not be so confusing to him. He may enjoy sitting down with you while you look at pictures in a book or read to him. This helps him with the task of speech and language acquisition. Remember, however, that your child's attention span is very short at this age. Let him go on to another activity rather than force him to sit with you.

He may show an interest in imitating you. This parrotlike imitation does not teach him anything about how to use the word or what it means. It will help him practice his pronunciation, though. If you teach him his body parts and clothing, he should easily recognize them when named. He may tell you what he wants by a combination of gestures and a few words. By the end of this stage, he may have built up a twenty-word vocabulary. Listen to him and give him a chance to add his own contribution, even if you cannot understand it. In return, you should talk to him to make him feel that he is a part of the family life, even if he cannot yet respond.

Physical Development

Your child is walking steadily; he seldom falls. In fact, he can walk backwards. He has begun to feed himself, even though he spills. Perhaps you have noticed his desire to climb all over objects — into chairs, up stairs, over tables. He helps undress himself by unzipping and removing some garments. With his hands he turns several pages at a time in a book. He can imitate your vertical strokes on paper with a crayon. By this age he is informing you of his toilet needs.

Checkpoints

Your eighteen-month-old child should be able to do the following:

Language and Speech Skills

(1) Recognize and point to some body parts.
(2) Name a few common household objects.
(3) Follow a simple command, such as "Put it on the chair."
(4) Identify a common picture, such as a dog.
(5) Ask for something by naming and pointing to it.
(6) Speak his own unintelligible jargon.
(7) Understand common short and simple sentences.
(8) Use one word to mean several things.

Physical Abilities

(1) Feed himself, even though he spills.
(2) Walk independently, and seldom fall.
(3) Walk backwards.
(4) Climb into a chair and climb stairs.
(5) Turn several pages at a time in a book.

   (6) Imitate vertical strokes with crayons.

   (7) Unzip and remove a single garment.

   (8) Tell you his toilet needs.

EIGHTEEN TO TWENTY-FOUR MONTHS CHILDREN'S CREATIVE WORD COMBINATIONS

THIS is the beginning of the speech "readiness" period. That is, your child has reached an appropriate maturational level for making speech sounds and creating simple word combinations of his own. Indeed, during this time period your child's spoken vocabulary reaches a level of as many as 300 words, he creates numerous word combinations of his own, and he displays a marked decrease in his use of jargon. Your child is experiencing an increased need for language to express all his new feelings and experiences. He uses words to ask for objects and to describe things around him.

Language Development

Your child learns the grammar of your language.

Your child is *ready* to learn the grammar of your language, whatever language it may be. Grammar represents the rules used to construct utterances. Thus, utterances are acceptable and meaningful to us if they conform to our well-learned grammatical rules. Utterances that do not conform to our grammatical rules appear nonsensical or ambiguous, such as "Under the dog black table is." It is believed that your child understands that grammatical relationships exist in the talk he hears, and he sets out to learn these relationships at this stage. He does this by being sensitive to the patterns and structures in your sentences. His mind may be set in a predetermined way to process these patterns, since he appears to pick up patterns when provided with only a few examples. The child who is entering this stage of development must bring, to some degree, the following skills with him in order to accomplish this task: (1) the ability to use symbols (words) to represent objects (that is, he recognizes that the word *water* refers to the clear liquid that we drink); (2) the ability to order the space around him (that is, he recognizes up from down, close from far, and he understands where he is in relationship to things around him); (3) the ability to understand time and sequence of events (he realizes that he went to bed last night and got up for breakfast later in the morning, even though he does not know the words to express it); (4) the ability to classify and categorize experiences and objects (he can group objects according to similar characteristics). If any of these skills are lacking or poorly developed, your child will have difficulty in the language-learning task.

How does your child tackle the problem of learning your grammar? First, he recognizes a language pattern in your speech. For example, he may notice that the subject or the doer of an action is mentioned first in sentence constructions. Then he formulates a rule for this observation which he uses to guide his own simple word combinations. He might say to you, "Daddy chair," to mean his father is sitting in the chair or it is his father's chair, rather than saying, "Chair Daddy."

The child generally makes an observation about some aspect of language, makes up a rule, and then applies it too broadly or to too many situations. That is, some applications of his rule are correct and some are incorrect. Your child is constantly going through a process of differentiating correct from incorrect forms. He may hear you say, "This is your*s*." From this he may deduce that both "this yours" and "this mines" are proper grammar according to his newly formed rule which adds *s* to the possessive pronouns. He must learn by listening to your speech that he has incorrectly applied the rule in one of these situations; his rule was too broad. He modifies his rule slightly, and then he scans your speech again to see if his rule is now the same as yours. It is obvious that your child will learn the language of his home faster if he has more interactions with you, and thus more experience with language.

Language becomes a useful tool for your child.

The first word combinations your child uses are probably learned as a unit and occur as if a single word. He says, "Go-bye-bye" or "Doggie-bark." He has not constructed or put these units together on his own, but rather has learned them as if they were one word. Your child proceeds from this stage to creating a few single two or three-word combinations on his own. This represents a major developmental advancement. He is beginning to create language of his own. Let us look closely at the nature and intent of his short little "sentences," keeping in mind that they are not imitative, but creative.

It is obvious from observing children's early word combinations that most children rely upon word order to express a grammatical relationship. Your child may say, "Mary sock," to mean, "This is Mary's sock." He may say, "Billy ball," to mean that Billy threw the ball. He uses word order and it has meaning. He does not say, "Ball Billy," but seems to respect the notion that words must be ordered, with subject first, then verb, and finally object, even though he may not yet use all these parts of speech.

Your child develops a language scheme.

From the very beginning, children organize and develop language schemes that respect rules of word class (a group of words that are used in the same way or place in sentences) and word order. Let us examine one such scheme in detail which is representative of this developmental stage. This scheme lays the foundation for the future development of your child's noun phrases. How is it that he comes to the point where he produces such a noun phrase as *My big car?* He does it by first developing two word classes. The first class is characterized by the following: (1) words other than nouns, (2) words that have a fixed position in an utterance, (3) words that do not occur alone, and (4) words that are slow to increase in number. There are not many words in this class, but they do include such words as *on, all gone, broken, big, pretty, my,* and *that.* Each child, of course, develops his own particular word class based on words he has a need for and has learned. In contrast, the second word class is characterized by the following: (1) Its words are mostly nouns; (2) the class is composed of many words; (3) it contains words that can occur alone with meaning; and (4) the words of the class are increasing in number all the time. Some examples of this word class are *milk, car, boy, sunshine, shoe, Mommy,* and *doggie.*

From these two classes your child constructs his two-word utterances. He produces combinations composed of words from his two word classes which are specific and are rule governed. They are not *random* combinations. Most of his combinations are made up from a word from the first word class followed by a word from the second word class, such as *big doggie, my car,* or *more milk.* However, other combinations occur also, such as *Mommy all gone, sock on,* or *Mommy sock.* He does not usually vary the order of the words in the combinations. The child does not, for example, say "Milk more"; he does not violate his own language scheme. However, his scheme is constantly undergoing change, almost too fast for description. The first word class divides eventually into four word classes: (1) articles, such as *a, the,* (2) demonstrative pronouns, such as *this, that,* (3) adjectives, such as *big, pretty,* and (4) possessive pronouns, such as *his, my* and *yours.* Now his scheme has become enough like yours to produce the noun phrase, *my big car.* He has word classes for *my, big,* and *car,* along with rules to prescribe their proper combination.

Your child, in his two or three-word utterances, is building a base for the nonsubject (predicate) part of a sentence, as well. The predicate is the part of the sentence which describes actions and which qualifies. You hear him say such things as, "See car," "Fall down," "No ride." In the next stage these units containing a verb are combined with the first two word classes used in building the noun phrase to form the basic simple sentence. But as yet, they are fragments of adult sentences. These verb combinations are ordered according to word position with the adverb or object usually following the verb, as in adult grammar.

Your child now begins to acquire the use of negating and questioning expressions.

His language forms are learned in a hierarchy of increasingly complex forms until they match the adult expressions. Your child no doubt by now has acquired that stubborn word *no* and is making use of it more often than you wish. To express negation, he will simply prefix his utterance with "no"; for example, "No go bed," or "No milk!" To ask a question, he does not yet make use of a question word but uses a rise in voice and pitch at the end of his sentence. As he becomes more sophisticated, he may tack a "what" or "where" onto the beginning of his utterance to ask a question.

You may wonder why your child's sentences are so short at this stage. Your child stores the rules for his grammar, and he stores the words. He has limited storage space (memory span) and formulation space in his brain at this young age. These physical traits limit his level of language competence. As his brain matures and his memory span increases, so do his language skills, if he has a stimulating home environment.

Your child finds his language useful in expressing many different ideas.

Even with his primitive language scheme your child can express an array of meanings. He can express the following: (1) nonexistence, "Milk all gone," (2) request, "More milk," (3) an object, "That ball," (4) notice of an object, "Hi, ball," (5) conjunctions, "Cup glass" (for "Here is a cup and a glass"), (6) an attribute of an object, "Pretty hat" (for "This is a pretty hat"), (7) possession, "My sock" (for "This is my sock"), (8) location, "Doggie door" (for "The dog is by the door"), and (9) subject-object relations, "Billy ball" (for "Billy threw the ball"). In general, children use subject-object word order before they learn and use the verb followed by the object or the subject-verb word order. Hence, your child is likely to say, "Billy ball" (to mean "Billy threw the ball") before saying

"Threw ball" or "Billy threw."

When we understand the child's language scheme, his sentences are more easily understood. However, even with this knowledge, we must rely on the situation at hand to be sure of the intent or meaning of the child's words. His speech usually reflects what he is doing or seeing at that moment. One comment, "Mommy sock," may mean mother has a sock in one instance, and in another mean that this is his mother's sock. Recall from Chapter 4 that the child's use of and meanings for individual words vary from that of yours.

Your child must learn how to make words.

At this stage, as we've seen, the child makes very little variation in the structure of the words he uses. For example, he does not yet know how to make *walked* or *walking* from the word *walk*. He learns one form of a word, usually the simplest form, before he learns and uses other forms of it. As with other types of language-learning, he will learn rules to govern such things as the addition of *-s, -ing,* or *-ed* to words. Once he knows how to add *-s* to a word, he does not have to learn such words as *cookie* and cookie*s* as two separate words. The rule determines the *form* of the word cookie*s*, and he thus does not have to learn it as a separate word.

Your child may be making up his own private words for things around him. His spoken vocabulary is increasing all the time. He has incorporated the use of the word *no* and it will soon lead to the variation *not*. He is also beginning to understand and perhaps use some of the different pronoun variations, such as *me, you,* and *mine*. He has much to learn in this phase of language development.

Your child understands more than he can say.

His understanding of language continues to be greater than what he can say himself. Although he does not use prepositions, he can understand some, such as *on, in,* and *under*. He also understands some of the pronouns, probably *me, mine,* and *you.* He is able to identify pictures when you say the name and can easily follow a command, such as, "Put the ball on the chair." Your child understands your sentences better if they are kept short and simple.

Speech Development

Your child is learning to say more consonants.

The child has two tasks when acquiring speech sounds. The first is that of perceiving the sound and its characteristics. That is, what makes one sound different from another speech sound. The second task is to develop the muscular coordination needed to produce the sound. Frequently, in early stages of sound acquisition, a child can hear the difference between, for instance, "candy" and "tandy" when you say it, but he still says "tandy" himself. Why is this? First, he may not have developed the necessary muscular control, and second, he may not know how to monitor his own sound production very well.

His speech as well as his language is developing. He now has the ability to use *p, m, h, n, w,* and *b* in several positions in a word. He recognizes the boundaries of these sounds. That is, he understands that *p* and *b* are two different sounds. He also has the muscular skill to say them with little or no distortion. You will notice that consonants used in the initial position are consistent, whereas the sounds in the remainder of the word may vary from time to time. For example, he may say "kwaku," "kwaka," or "kwaker" to mean *cracker.* Sound substitutions are quite frequent in his speech. He may be heard to say "witto" for *little,* "wed" for *red,* as well as "thip" for *sip* or for *zip.* If you are around the child often you can decipher the sounds he distorts or substitutes, but other persons may find him incomprehensible at first.

The melody and flow of your child's speech changes as he develops.

Repetitions in the speech flow are characteristic of the early vocalizations and speech of young children. The number of repetitions in the child's speech is greatest at about one year of age and then decreases. The repetitious nature of the child's speech is considered to be a *normal* occurrence in the developmental process.

Your child may also repeat words or rhyming words in a songlike pattern. He appears to enjoy playing with words. He may also enjoy expressing different emotions in his play and while talking with you.

Parental Guidelines

You are a teacher of speech and language.

You may discover that your child loves to hear a simple story over and over again. This is good language learning for him. He may enjoy sitting with you while looking and talking about pictures in a book. Talk about the pictures or make up a simplified version of the story rather than reading directly from the book. Storytelling and reading all through the preschool years is good language-learning practice. Your child may imitate you, a form of playing. Give him practice in following directions. Play together, work together, talk together. Your child needs experience, to go places and to see new things. An ever expanding and exciting world creates the need for the expansion of his language and speech abilities. Your child no doubt has a repertoire of cute words or phrases. Enjoy them yourself but do not pressure him to perform for others; he has not yet acquired the skills and confidence to become a performer.

Some practices are not necessarily helpful to your child's language learning at this age, even though they might seem as though they would be. Imitating you is not likely to teach meaningful communication. It can be fun for both you and your child. It is a form of play rather than a form of instruction in language learning. If a parent continually corrects a child's grammar without paying attention to what the message is, the parent will soon undermine the communication process. You, as a parent, should first respond to what it is that your child is attempting to tell you. It is vitally important to your child that you be a good listener. Communication attempts should be cherished and rewarded, since your child has much to learn and cannot be expected to acquire it all at once. He should not be discouraged when he is just beginning the language-learning process, but he should be given much support from you in the form of praise.

Physical Development

Your child is developing in other areas, too.

Your child's language and speech develop *as a result* of maturational processes and continued new experiences. So do his physical abilities. Physical development takes place alongside the speech and language development. A deficit in physical development is often accompanied by a delay in language development. We all know that different children develop at different rates, but the relationship between the physical and language abilities remains relatively constant. If your child is doing well in one respect, he will normally be doing well in the other.

Your child can jump in place, run quite well, kick a large ball, and walk up stairs, two feet per step. With his hands, he can scribble with a crayon or build a block tower. He is not quite old enough to be toilet trained, but he understands what you want him to do on the toilet.

It is important to note that although the aspects of speech and language development detailed in this chapter are described separately, they are in fact occurring simultaneously in your child. Many things are changing and advancing at once, as they should be, for he is ready for them. We know, too, that there is much variability from child to child in speech and language acquisition. Keep this fact in mind when observing your child's developmental pattern. In a few short years, your child learns the language of his community through complex and fast-changing language schemes. Let us now see how these schemes continue to develop into adult language and speech patterns now that the processes have been activated in the young child.

Checkpoints

Your twenty-four-month-old child should be able to do the following:

Language and Speech Skills

(1) Remember two consecutive digits.
(2) Use two or three-word combinations.
(3) Understand a few prepositions.
(4) Understand some common personal pronouns: *me, mine, you.*
(5) Express negation by the use of "no."
(6) Produce *p, m, n, b, w,* and *h* correctly in words in the initial position.
(7) Ask for something using the word as well as gestures.

Physical Abilities

(1) Run well.
(2) Kick a large ball.
(3) Build a block tower.
(4) Scribble with a crayon.
(5) Walk up stairs, two feet per step.
(6) Hold a small glass in one hand.
(7) Remove shoes that are unlaced.
(8) Find and insert an arm into the armhole of a garment.
(9) Know what is expected when placed on the toilet.

TWO TO THREE YEARS
THE FIRST COMPLETE SENTENCE

YOUR child makes remarkable advances in language and vocabulary during this period. By three years of age he will be expressing many of his ideas and desires in complete sentences, three to four words in length. You will understand most of what your child says to you. His vocabulary makes a larger relative increase in size than it ever will again. It triples, reaching nearly 900 words. He will have command of the basic simple sentence structure, which includes a noun, a verb, and an object. The simple sentence is the heart of the language and that structure from which we create more complex language forms. The next year will find him a competent citizen of his language community.

Language Development

Let us examine first how your child advances from his many two to three-word combinations through to the basic simple sentence structure. During this phase his word order and grammar may not necessarily match that of yours. It is, however, produced in accordance with his current language scheme, which means that his utterances are governed by his own system of grammatical rules.

Your child continues the process of rule formation and rule-testing in order to develop complete sentences.

The noun phrases and verb phrases are developing from his language scheme of two to three-word combinations. As the maturational process proceeds, the child's ability to remember and formulate language increases. Thus he approaches the stage at which he has both the raw material — noun and verb phrases — and the mental capability to join the phrases together to form a complete sentence.

The noun phrases are well developed and may resemble the following phrases: "My big car," "The pretty doggie," "A good girl," and "That shoe." The verb phrases, also well-developed, are combinations such as, "Ride in car," "See pretty birdie," "Fall down hurt, Mommy," and "Put on chair." Your child previously used combinations of either subject followed by the object of the sentence, or the verb followed by the object.

Your child now combines the noun and verb phrases to produce utterances such as, "The car broken," "That my toy," "It a cow," "Me a good boy," or "Me in bed, Mommy." As you notice, these are not quite complete sentences; some verb forms must still be added. This is the final step leading to the creation of a complete sentence. Now, your child adds the verb *is* and other action verbs in the present tense to his utterances.

Even though your child develops a complete sentence with subject, verb, and object, it contains some mistakes in grammar. Your child is likely to say, "It not me," "Lemme do again," "Dat book is mines," or "I see birdie."

During this stage of development the simple sentences your child uses may sound "telegraphic" to you. He may have left out the smaller, less stressed words in the sentence much as we would do in order to conserve space when sending a telegram. Perhaps your child is also conserving space by leaving out such words as prepositions (*in, on*), helping verbs (*am, is, will, are*), and conjunctions (*and, but*) which do not carry as much information and meaning. Your child incorporates any language form that you frequently use into his own scheme. If you swear often, he is likely to do the same. If the language form is too complex for his level of development, he will render his own version of it and use it in the appropriate situation.

It is amazing indeed to realize that your child deduces the rules of grammar by hearing only a few examples from your speech. He is never exposed to the rule system itself, but only the examples. We, as adults, operate according to rule systems, too, but we would not be able to state the rules we use in speaking; speech and language either sound correct and make sense or are recognized as incorrect. We make these judgments in accordance with our system of rules. Your child must develop the same skill regarding speech and language and the rules which govern them.

Your child is fascinated by new words.

Your child's language is becoming more complex and more useful to him all the time. He has discovered a need for more vocabulary words, partly because he realizes that he has overextended many of his early-learned words. For example, all four-legged creatures, he learns, are not in fact dogs. He now needs the names for cats, cows, and horses. This same principle applies to many other first-learned words. Now he is acquiring the meaning of a word that more closely resembles the meaning which you attach to the word. At first your child is confused by different words that have similar meanings.

The increase in vocabulary parallels his increase in questioning behavior and the reduction in the overextension of his vocabulary words. He understands the magic of words, is curious about what things are called, and now knows that words make up sentences. The power of language is no longer a mystery, but is becoming a tool for him. It is up to you to help your child during this period of rapid vocabulary growth. You can step in and supply your child with the new vocabulary words when he needs them or asks for them. He may discover a new object or realize that his word is inappropriate for an old object. You supply the word at this point. At an earlier stage, he was not interested or ready to learn so many new words. You can help him to apply labels to his feelings, as well. He needs to express happiness, sadness, anger, and fear, just as you do.

Your child begins to learn how to vary the structure of his words.

Your child now begins to vary the structure and form of his newly acquired vocabulary words. He develops specific rules which determine these word variations. Again, these rules may not be the same as yours. For example, he acquires the rule to add *s* to nouns to produce such words as *mouses, feets,* and *peoples.* He applies his rule too broadly.

As we noted in the last chapter, your child expressed negation by simply prefixing his statement with *no.* At this age he will move *no* into the sentence in front of the verb. He begins to use the word form *not* to express negation. He states to you, "It not pretty," "Me not do it," "He no bite you," or "There no birds outside."

You will now see evidence of progress in this aspect of language acquisition, because he not only varies the form of nouns by adding an *s,* but he learns also how to make variations on the verb tenses that he uses. When he first used verbs, he made use only of the verb *is* and some other present tense action verbs: "It's my book," "Me want the ball," or "Mommy take shoe." Now he learns to add *-ing* to verbs and to use the past tense verb forms to express "I going too, Mommy," "The big doggie running," or "The ball fell downstairs."

As he is acquiring rules for his word forms, an interesting variation of verb tenses may occur. Your child may use the proper forms, such as *fell* or *threw* for irregular past tense verbs, or such forms as *gonna, wanna,* or *hafta* in his sentences. He learns these forms from listening to your speech. At this stage, your child acquires the rule to add *-ed* to all verbs to indicate past tense. He determines the rule from the pattern he notices in your speech. Unlike you, however, he applies his rule to *every* verb. Therefore, you hear him begin to use "falled" and "throwed" where he previously used the proper forms. This is confusing, even upsetting to many parents. Your child, of course, has simply applied his language rule too broadly, as we have often seen him do. Obviously, he did not hear "falled" or "throwed" in your speech, but generated them himself. However, he will discover in his own time that his rule does not apply to certain situations and will make allowances for this in his language scheme. This may occur with other parts of speech, as well.

Your child increases the number of different pronouns, prepositions, and question words in his speech. He may use the following pronoun forms: *me, mine, you,* and *I.* However, he may use some of these forms incorrectly at this stage of acquisition. The prepositions *in, on,* and *under* may also occur in his speech. He begins to incorporate question words into his vocabularly in the following order: *what, what do ..., where, whose,* and *who.* These words allow him to gain valuable information about his world and to produce more sophisticated sentences. Typical speech examples are "What you doing?" "What dat man do?" "Where my sock go?", etc. He has much to learn about the formation and use of the various word forms. In the next stage he will make many advancements in this area of language development.

How much does your child understand at this age?

Your child understands most adult sentences now. If you give him a series of two short commands he can carry them out. He can answer more thought-provoking questions, such as, "What do we do when we are sleepy?" If you ask him to give you just *one* block, he will. He understands the number concept (see glossary) of one versus many. He recognizes the function of many common household objects and can identify simple actions in pictures. He begins to understand the prepositions *beside, in front of,* and *behind.* He now knows the difference between such adjectives as *big/little, fast/slow,* or *long/short.* He recognizes some basic colors. An increasing memory span adds to his ability to comprehend. At this stage he should be able to repeat after you a series of three digits, such as 9-4-7. He repeats one more digit now than he did in the previous stage.

Speech Development

Your child is developing his speech sounds, too.

You have probably observed your child playing with words. His articulation is faulty. His speech flow may be characterized by hesitations, and sound, syllable, or word repetitions. This is considered a *normal* occurrence in speech and language development. His voice control is not perfected yet, and his voice ranges from loud to soft when speaking. He may sometimes rhyme long strings of words, changing consonants and vowels one at a time. For example, he may say, *pee, poo, pa, pie,* or *housie, lousie, mousie, pousie.* He adds sounds to familiar words and creates his own new words. He does this because he has discovered that words are composed of individual sounds. He recognizes speech sounds, or letters of the alphabet, as unique, each with its own distinctive sound boundaries. Previously, your child may not have been sure when one sound ended and another started — speech was one continuous flow of sound to his ears. If now you were to ask him if *bear* and *pear* were the same, he would say no, because he can now hear the difference between *b* and *p*.

This discovery that words are composed of individual sounds helps him to improve his pronunciation. He can be understood easily by those outside the family circle, even though his pronunciation is not perfect. He can now use the following consonants with ease: *p, m, h, n, w, b, k, g, d, t,* and *-ng.* His sound system is becoming more specific and complete. In earlier stages, you will recall, he used one sound in the place of many.

What makes a particular word more difficult for your child to say?

A word can be difficult if it does any or all of the following: (1) contains many syllables, *tel-e-vi-sion,* (2) contains late-learned sounds, *squirrel,* (3) is an unfamiliar word, *lingerie,* or (4) contains consonant clusters, *stripe.* When a word is too difficult for him, your child may omit letters, or, at a later stage, substitute a similar sound for that sound he cannot make, such as "dat" for *that,* "bwover" for *brother,* or "wight" for *light.* A sound may be learned at a later age if it requires more complex muscle movements, is not easily seen on the lips, or if it contains more subtle sound features.

Your child builds his sound system by learning sounds.

English is made up of many different sounds, each with its own characteristics. Some sounds, or as we usually refer to them, letters, sound similar to one another. Your child must learn to produce, combine, and differentiate all of the sounds in our language. This enables him to understand that sounds differ from one another. Sounds are made to differ from one another by varying the positions of the mouth and by changes in the breath stream. He acquires his own set of rules to govern his production of sounds. Thus he builds his own sound system. He bases this sound system upon the information he receives from the speech around him. He will appear to speak poorly if his system differs very much from yours. As he matures and gains experience in speaking and listening, his sound system acquires more rules of the adult sound system. This makes his speech more acceptable to you. Let us now follow an example of a typical rule that a child may formulate at this age.

Your child forms a rule for speech.

Consider the sound that the letter *f* makes. This is a difficult sound for children to produce. It involves many complex muscle movements. At this age your child may not be able to perceive all of the characteristics inherent in the production of the *f* sound, and he may not be able to coordinate muscle movements when needed to produce the *f*. He knows, however, that one must say a consonant sound in the beginning of the word *finger*. What he does, in this case, is to pick a consonant with a sound similar to one that he already knows he *can* produce to substitute for the *f* sound. He would probably pick the *p* and/or *t* sounds to represent the *f* sound in his speech. Thus he has formed a rule that says: *f* equals *p* and/or *t* in the initial position of a word. So he may say "pinger" for *finger*, or "tish" for *fish*. As the child begins to perceive more characteristics of the *f* sound, he determines that it is indeed a separate sound than either *p* or *t*. At this point he tries different combinations of muscle movements to try to reproduce the new sound until he discovers what it takes to make the *f* sound properly. He now has a rule that says that *f* is composed of certain characteristics. These characteristics are the same as yours, so he can now pronounce words beginning with *f* just like you do, and he discards his old rule, *f* equals *p* and/or *t*.

As you have probably noticed, some children seem to speak clearly, with only a few substitutions or distortions in words almost from the time they begin speaking. Other children still seem to have substitutions for missing sounds in the first grade. This is because there is a great deal of variability in the rate of acquisition of speech sounds from child to child. Table I, "The Acquisition of Speech Sounds," gives the ages by which speech pathologists feel a child should have mastered a certain sound. Many children will master sounds earlier, of course, than is indicated in Table I. The most important point for you to understand is that your child speaks clearly when his own nerve centers and speech musculature are sufficiently developed, *and not before*. Therefore, a child should not be made to suffer shame or be pressured when he cannot say words properly. He needs loving support from you, not disappointment, disapproval, or laughter.

Parental Guidelines

How can you best help him with his speech sounds?

You can help your child with his pronunciation. *When* to help is as important as *how* to help. There are certain times when correction may not be appropriate. When your child is excited and very intent on his message, do not interrupt him with a correction. Instead, listen to his message. If there is much noise, commotion, or excitement about, do not bother your child with corrections. If you must correct your child's pronunciation, do it when there are few distractions and when he is not too excited to listen to what you say. Remember, however, that there is nothing to be gained in correcting him all the time. Rather, if correction is necessary, choose a time or two during the day that is relatively peaceful and quiet. Perhaps during story time, or when reading together you can help him with new words.

How you correct your child's pronunciation is very important, too. It is important not to be negative about your child's speaking attempts. Correct his pronunciation in a friendly, positive manner. That is, *do not* say, "No, Jimmy, say 'cat,' not 'tat.'" Instead, you might intercede after he says, "Look, a tat," and say, "cat," or "Yes, that is a cat," with slight emphasis on "cat." Give him a chance to hear how you say the word when it is not buried within a flow of speech. Parents have found it helpful to teach their children to correct themselves by example. One mother would purposely make a mistake in her pronunciation, then say out loud, "No, that's not quite right," and then repeat the word correctly. The child learns two lessons from this. First, he learns that even grownups make mistakes, so he is not alone in making errors. Second, he learns a procedure for self-correction. Your child must not be made to feel that his mistakes are wrong or bad. After all, at this point his language and sound system are merely different from yours.

You can help your child with his language, too.

You should be aware of possible teaching techniques used in language stimulation and correction. There are essentially five methods. Using the first method, you merely correct the child. For example, he says, "He satted on the chair." You reply, "He *sat* on the chair." This method is less positive or constructive than the following methods, but certainly puts an emphasis on correct grammar. In the second method, you expand the child's sentence. Your child says, "Dog barking," and you reply, "Yes, the dog *is* barking." This is good help for improving the child's sentence structure. The third method is one of building upon the child's idea. He says to you, "Dog barking," and you reply, "Yes, dogs bark and people talk." You are helping him to understand the world around him. The fourth method is to keep his ideas going by your comments. Your child says to you, "See birds." You reply by asking, "Where?" He then tells you, "On roof." You keep the topic going by adding more information or saying something like, "What are they doing?" or "Which birds do you like?" You add some information or comment upon everything that your child says regarding the birds. The last approach is that of asking questions which force the child to think of a reply. For example, he says, "Dog barking," and you say, "Yes, how can you tell?"

You can stimulate your child's language learning by some less specific actions as well. At this age your child benefits from a special time each day when you and he read a book together or listen to stories on records or tapes. He can understand and listen to much longer stories now. Undoubtedly he has some favorite stories that he likes to hear over and over again. These exercises help to focus his attention on listening, and thereby improve this skill as well. If your child watches a television program, ask him questions about what he sees. Talk about the shows. Some children's programs are designed to stimulate language learning.

In conversations with your child, you should both take turns listening and speaking. It is still a good idea for you to talk to him about what he is doing, what you are doing, and what is happening around the house. Painting, pasting, and coloring are good activities for increasing his language concepts. He needs continual interaction with things and people in his environment in order to continue to learn. As the child's age approaches three years, you may want to call his attention to different shapes, such as circles, squares, and triangles, as well as a few colors. He may enjoy naming and matching colors and shapes, which may also be used to help him develop number concepts. You can teach him his first and last name. It is handy for him to know his address, too, in case he gets lost!

A word of warning to parents.

The young preschool child is prone to use his voice to its loudest, for imitating his favorite animal, shouting, or pretending that he is a logging truck. The child may want to identify himself with his parents by trying to talk in a high pitch like his mother, or a low pitch like his father. Any of these behaviors, if repeated day after day, may cause damage to his vocal cords. Growths may form on the vocal cords that may prevent them from closing properly. The voice then sounds hoarse, too shrill, or breathy. These growths will disappear if the abusive behavior is discontinued. However, it takes only a small amount of any type of voice abuse per day to maintain the growths, once they have formed on the vocal cords. If the child's voice makes a noticeable change that lasts for more than two weeks, he should be checked by an ear, nose, and throat specialist. Listen to your child during his play. Is he shouting, making noises unnatural for his speaking voice, or straining his voice in any other manner much of the time? If so, this could explain the noticeable change in his voice. If these behaviors seem to be causing a voice change, they should be discouraged.

Physical Development

Your child, while acquiring the language and speech skills mentioned above, will also have developed the following physical skills. He can ride a tricycle, catch a ball, and stand on one foot for one second. His more refined physical abilities include building a nine or ten-block tower, or copying a circle and a horizontal line on paper. He can undress himself (with a little help from you). He eats without spilling most of the time, and uses a fork to eat with. He is toilet trained and can manage on the toilet with a little help from you in cleansing.

As mentioned earlier, these are average abilities. Some children mature fast, others more slowly. Recall that whether the developmental process is fast or slow, the patterns of speech, language, and physical development remain relatively constant with respect to one another. See Table II, "Physical and Speech Milestones Parallel Each Other," for a summary of the correlation of the developmental patterns.

Tᴀʙʟᴇ II

PHYSICAL AND SPEECH MILESTONES PARALLEL EACH OTHER

AGE	*PHYSICAL SKILLS*	*SPEECH & LANGUAGE SKILLS*
6 Months	sits	babbles
12 Months	stands, walks	uses first words, understands some words
18 Months	walks steadily	jargon sounds like adult sentences
24 Months	runs	two or three-word utterances, babbling decreases
30 Months	jumps with both feet, stands on one foot, builds block tower	understands most adult sentences. Utterances three words or more
36 Months	stands on tiptoes	responses fairly complete, grammatical errors decrease
54 Months	hops on one foot	language is developed

Checkpoints

Your three-year-old child should be able to do the following:

Speech and Language Skills

(1) Talk, using some complete sentences three to four words in length.
(2) Use some pronouns and prepositions.
(3) Use *what* in addition to one or two more question words.
(4) Form a negative sentence.
(5) Use both present and past tense verbs.
(6) Know many new vocabulary words.
(7) Pronounce the following consonants correctly: *p, b, w,*

m, n, h, t, d, -ng, k, and *g.*

(8) Repeat one series of digits: 1-8-3.

(9) Understand most adult sentences.

Physical Abilities

(1) Stand on tiptoe or balance on one foot for one second.

(2) Ride a tricycle.

(3) Catch a ball.

(4) Copy a circle and horizontal line.

(5) Build a nine or ten-block tower.

(6) Undress himself with help on fastenings.

(7) Unlace his shoes.

(8) Use a fork without spilling.

(9) Manage on the toilet with help in cleansing.

THREE TO FOUR YEARS
A FLOOD OF QUESTIONS

As your child reaches this stage in language development, he not only talks a lot, but he follows you around constantly, asking ceaseless questions. Your child is trying out his newly acquired speech and language skills, obtaining information about an increasingly exciting world, and in general using questions to make you talk to him more. You can reason verbally with your child at this age. His sentences are approximately five to six words in length. His improved memory allows him to tell you stories with sequential events and to recall past events accurately. He uses speech both to command and to demand something from his parents and peers. His vocabulary is in excess of 1500 words, but do not expect him to talk like an adult who, like yourself, has a vocabulary of 12,000 to 13,000 words.

Language Development

It is at this stage of language development that parents generally begin to expect greater excellence in their child's speech. You may now begin to compare your child's speech and language to your own. This is because the child has developed an observable level of competence in his speech and language skills. Parents need to remember, however, that their children have not completed the task of speech and language learning. Therefore, children's speech must be evaluated accordingly.

An understanding of grammatical complexity helps you to understand developmental order.

When we consider grammatical complexity, we can look at

two aspects. First, we can determine the type and complexity of the sentence. Second, we can determine the level of complexity of the various parts of speech within that sentence, such as the nouns, pronouns, or verbs. The order in which your child develops language does not strictly follow the scale of increasing grammatical complexity because there are other factors involved. For example, your child tends at some point to incorporate those language forms he hears most often in your speech, so there is not always a one-to-one correspondence between developmental schemes and schemes of increasing grammatical complexity. The two schemes, however, are relatively similar in that the child generally learns less complex grammar first.

The simplest sentence is one that merely makes an affirmative statement: *I see the horse.* The sentence becomes more complex if it is in question form: *Did you see the horse?* To make the sentence negative increases the complexity even more: *I did not see the horse.* To continue to make the sentence increasingly more complex, include a negation *and* a question: *Didn't you see the horse?* Then we can switch to passive verb tense and go through the above sequence with all these forms being even more complex than the examples above. For further examples, refer to Table III, "Developmental Sentence Types." Passive tense is more complex because the doer of the action follows, rather than precedes the verb, which deviates from common word order: *I was hit* by the ball. To continue with the scheme of increasing complexity you then proceed to sentences which contain phrases or conjunctions within them, such as these two: He is the man *who came over yesterday,* or I brought the gift *because it was his birthday.*

The complexity of the parts of speech, such as verbs, pronouns, conjunctions, and question words may also be determined. An understanding of the increasing complexity of verbs will be noted in Table III, "Developmental Verb Forms." The addition of various auxiliary verbs (*is, are, will,* etc.) makes the verb forms even more complex. Such indefinite pronouns as *it, that,* and *this* are less complex than *both, few,* or *some,* because these latter words require an additional understanding of number concepts. Such pronouns as *you, me, I, he,* and *she* are learned much sooner than *myself, himself,* and *theirs.*

If you have a feeling for levels of grammatical complexity, it can help you to better understand and follow the sequence of your child's language development. It can explain why he does not understand what you said, or why he may be making certain errors — the forms were too complex for his level of development. Let us look at some of the grammatical forms of a child of this age.

Your child expands his grammar rules as his memory span increases.

As your child grows, his brain and nervous system mature. This allows him to understand and create more complex language forms as well as increase his memory span. He is able to express more complicated thoughts by the use of many different sentence types. The complicated thoughts and complex language forms require more steps to formulate them, and require the application of more rules in a set order to produce an utterance that is grammatically correct. Thus he needs to increase his memory span and concept formation in order to tackle the particular problems that each stage of language and speech development present to him.

Your child is able to use interrogative (int.), imperative (imp.), declarative (dec.), and negative sentences. Some typical sentences of this age group might include the following: *I see a blue book* (dec.), *They sleeping in their beds* (dec.), *What name you're writing* (int.), *I don't know what him doing* (neg.), *I been there* (dec.), *This can't go* (neg.), *That's not my shoe* (neg.), and *Give me a cookie* (imp.). The sentences are longer and include more complex forms even though they are not always completely correct. Your child has the ability to ask more complicated questions. At this stage he also incorporates the use of another style of asking questions — those that require only a yes or no answer. This involves the inversion of the subject and the verb. These will be discussed in detail later.

These language forms are more complex because they require

Table III

DEVELOPMENTAL FORMS DISPLAYING
INCREASED GRAMMATICAL COMPLEXITY

Developmental Verb Forms[1]

1. I play. It is good. It's good.
2. He play. She play. It play.
3. I playing. He playing.
4. I is playing. You is playing.
5. He is playing.
6. He plays. He played.
7. I am playing. He was playing.
8. We are good. They were good.
9. I can play. He will play.
10. I don't play. They don't play.
11. Do you play? Do they play?
12. They do play.
13. He could play. He would play.
14. He might play. He should play.
15. He doesn't play. He didn't play.
16. Does he play? Did he play?
17. He does play. He did play.
18. I must play. I shall play. (rare)
19. I have eaten. I had eaten.
20. The music was being played.
21. The music could have been played.
22. I have been playing.
23. I may have eaten.
24. I might be playing.
25. I might have been playing.

Developmental Sentence Forms[2]

1. I see the horse.
2. Did you see the horse?
3. I did not see the horse.
4. Didn't you see the horse?
5. The horse was seen by me.
6. Was the horse seen by you?
7. The horse was not seen by me.
8. Wasn't the horse seen by you?
9. I brought the gift, because it was his birthday.
10. He is the man who came over yesterday.

[1]Adapted in part from L. Lee and S. Canter, "Developmental Sentence Scoring: A Clinical Procedure for Estimating Syntactic Development in Children's Spontaneous Speech," *Journal of Speech and Hearing Disorders, 31*:311-330, 1966.
[2]Courtesy of R. Brown and C. Hanlon, "Derivation Complexity and Order of Acquisition in Child Speech," in J. Hayes (ed.), *Cognition and the Development of Language* (New York, Wiley, 1970).

a more advanced level of cognitive development to be understood and used properly.

In all children cognitive development and word learning are intricately interwoven.

As with other facets of language learning, cognitive development plays a central role in acquiring adult meaning for words. Developing the meaning of a word is a problem of concept formation for the child. It is a problem because he hears a word used in a variety of situations and from this he must determine what the characteristics of that word are, and in what situations that word is used. For example, he must learn all of the various objects that we refer to as brushes: clothes brush, toothbrush, hair brush, and scrub brush. He forms a category for *brush*. He does the same thing with other words, like *furniture*. The concept of furniture, and thus its meaning, is developed by learning all the different things that make up furniture. Your child is acquiring the adult meanings for words at this stage.

Your child first formulates a personal definition for a word — a definition that relates directly to his own experience. Thus, a *red dress* may only be the type of red dress his mother wears, and not just any red dress. As he reaches this stage, though, he develops meanings that are more general and are shared by the rest of his language community. Eventually, a *red dress* becomes any red dress to him, too.

This entire process of acquiring adult word meaning takes much longer than all the other facets of speech and language development. Development in this aspect of language continues to at least eleven years of age. It is a slow process for three reasons. First, it depends upon intellectual maturity. Second, words have many definitions and wide variation in use. Third, no rule dictates why a word is what it is, and therefore a word meaning is an abstract concept, difficult to grasp.

Your child will acquire the word for objects and situations that you supply for him. These are usually words that are most useful to the child at the time. You may teach him, for example, that a coin is a *penny* rather than *currency*. You probably will identify yourselves as *Mama* and *Daddy* rather than *parents* to your young child. Vocabulary growth for the child proceeds in general from concrete words to more abstract words. For example, your child generally uses the words *table* and *chair* before he uses the word *furniture* in making reference to those objects. Conceptually, your child gradually makes more and more distinctions in his world, thus forming more categories which require more vocabulary words. For example, your child probably learns the word *fish* before he learns that there are many different types of fish, each with a different name.

Your child has become quite sophisticated in varying the structure of words.

As with other areas in language development, your child learns to vary the structure of more of his vocabulary words. He began by merely adding an *s* to nouns. He has now acquired and can use the following forms: (1) plurals on nouns, hat*s*, (2) regular past tense verbs, turn*ed*, (3) possessives on nouns, using *'s*, Mommy*'s* hat, (4) the third person singular verb form that requires an *s*, he want*s*, the dog run*s*, and (5), the *-ing* ending with auxiliary verb, she *is* go*ing* with us. At this stage your child still thinks that all nouns can exist in both singular and plural forms, merely by the addition of an *s* to the singular form. His rule is still too general. You still hear *feets* and *mouses*. He regularly produces forms not heard in your speech, but this is a progression for him, not a regression. He still adds *-ed* to some irregular verb forms to produce such words as *wented, hitted,* or *sitted,* even though he correctly handles the verbs that require an *-ed* ending. At this early date there is no reason for endless correcting of your child's grammar. Be a good language model. Let him hear the proper forms in your speech often, and he will in time correct himself.

He expresses negation now by attaching *not* to the auxiliary verbs *can, do,* and *did* to form sentences containing *can't, didn't, don't, cannot,* etc. Before he was able to make this advancement, he had to learn the auxiliary verbs and their proper usage. The use of the auxiliary verbs allows your child to formulate more complex and accurate verb tenses in his sentences.

He uses the *I* pronoun instead of *me,* and *my* instead of *mines* at this stage. His use and understanding of pronouns more closely match that of an adult. At this stage he is more likely to say, "He has my shoes," rather than, "Him gots mine shoe."

Your child's ability to use questions is advancing.

Your child's increase in questioning behavior is obvious, and so is his ability to ask more complicated questions. As you recall, your child first makes use of such question words as *what, what do, whose,* and *who.* To these he now adds the following forms: *where...from, why, how,* and *when.* In the beginning of questioning behavior, your child just tacked these *wh* question words onto the front of a sentence, such as "What you doing, Mommy?" Now he begins to say "What *are* you doing, Mommy?" He is becoming more sophisticated in his grammar. Instead of asking, "Where book is?" he says, "Where is the book?" Note that he has made use of newly learned auxiliary verbs in his question forms, too.

He is also developing another style of asking questions — those which only require yes or no as an answer. To ask a yes/no question, the verb and subject are inverted and the addition of the word *do* is required in some places. The following questions illustrate this: "Can't I go play?" "Did you see birds?" "Does the dog sits up?" "Are you coming?" This question style develops later than others because it involves an inversion of usual word order as well as more complicated auxiliary verb forms such as *are, did, does, can,* etc.

When your child has reached this level of questioning ability, he can answer most of your questions properly, which he was not able to do before. When he first began asking you "why" questions, he probably did not understand what he was asking, nor did he understand your "why" questions. Your child asks questions to gain information, but many of his questions serve different purposes. He may use them as ways to get your attention. When he merely makes a statement to you, you mumble, "uh huh," but when he asks you a question, you turn to him and supply an answer. He has thus successfully engaged you in conversation. He asks questions he knows the answer to as a way of beginning a conversation with adults. In this last instance, you may try answering your child's question with one of your own. He seems to want the language drill that endless questioning behavior supplies him with.

Your child comprehends new language concepts.

Your child gains valuable information about his world through experience. He then is able to relate this by means of his language. If he has no understanding of things around him, he does not need to develop the language to talk about it.

Your child can answer such questions as, "What do you do when you are sleepy, hungry, or cold?" or "What do we do with our eyes, ears, or mouth?" He can identify an object by function, such as, "Which one do we eat with?" He understands the number concept of both *one* and *two*. If you ask him to bring you two cookies, he does it. He may be able to count, but it is usually merely rote memorization, without grasp of the number concept. He can name and recognize some of the primary colors. He understands more prepositions, such as *by, between, in front of,* and *beside.* He has a firm understanding for past, present, and future events, and knows that these require different verb tenses. The sense of time is one of the more difficult concepts your child must master. He is beginning to develop a sense of time as implied by verb tenses. In our modern society and in our language, time is an important concept. Do not be surprised when the words *yesterday* and *tomorrow* confuse him; he will still be confused by time-related words. Minutes, hours, weeks, months, and years are all measures of time that elude the young preschool child. This is the reason why the question word *when* is the last to be acquired by the child — it relates to time.

Speech Development

Your child's pronunciation improves, too.

At this stage your child begins to produce some of the more difficult consonants, such as the *ch-, j, sh-,* and *v.* These consonants may not be perfected, but he attempts to make them. He may be more handy with the newly added sounds of *f, y, r, l,* and *s.* You may find that your child enjoys rhymes and nonsense syllables. He enjoys playing with sounds and words; it's a method for perfecting his pronunciation.

Hesitations and repetitions are natural in the speech flow during this stage.

This stage, the three to four-year-old period, is a critical one for the child in learning to keep the speech flow of his utterance smooth flowing. You may notice that his speech is characterized by a large number of hesitations, restarts, rephrases, and repetitions. These interruptions in his speech flow are part of the normal course of speech development. Some children naturally will display more interruptions in their speech flow than others. In fact, studies show that boys have more repetitions in their speech than girls. The preschool child's speech contains more interruptions in the form of sound and syllable repetitions and stallers (*um, ah, uh*) than any other form of interruption.

The interruptions in your child's speech are not associated with any struggle or tension in speaking. He is not frustrated by these interruptions and even appears not to be aware that they exist in his speech. This is good, since smooth speech flow is just another hurdle in the task of acquiring speaking skills.

You may be more aware of the interruptions in your child's speech at this age, however. You may ask yourself why they exist. Actually, your child has fewer interruptions in his speech now than he did during previous stages. Children's repetitions tend to diminish with increasing age during the preschool period. It is at about this age when parents begin to compare their child's speech to their own adult standards of speech, and thus notice more of the errors and interruptions. Your child has only recently acquired his speech and language skills; therefore he should not be expected to have the facility of an adult. He must have time to perfect the flow of speech in his utterances as with everything else. Certainly we should not label a child a "stutterer" for the interruptions in his speech at this age.

Let us look at the interruptions and some of the situations in which they are likely to occur, as well as why. Your child may repeat a sound (*s-s-sammy*), a syllable (*la-la-lady*), or a word (*the-the-the*). He may hesitate before the next word in the sentence, saying, "uh, uh, uh, Mary did that." He may start the sentence over halfway through it or decide to rephrase it. He may prolong one sound longer than ordinary, such as *mmmmommy*.

A child may hesitate when trying to express a complex message, to recall the word he wants to use, or to tell the order of events correctly. This is no different from what we adults do, but we just do not do it as often. We are more skilled in our speaking ability. The child has many things to communicate to you now, all of which seem very important to him. A child may feel that what he has to say is not important, if adults are not good listeners. He may then hesitate or repeat, in a debate as to whether he should speak or not. If a child is angry, frightened, or upset, his speaking ability may be affected. If he is very excited about something, he may try to relate his message faster than he has the ability to, and his speech may break down. If your child thinks he will be interrupted, he may try to speak faster than his ability allows, in order to try to keep the floor. This, too, may result in speech interruptions. If your child has to compete with better speakers to get a word into the conversation, the pressure of the situation may cause him to repeat or hesitate. The child may, in certain situations, use hesitations or repetitions to irritate his parents or to demand their attention. Something upsetting in the family environment, such as a new baby, moving to a new location, or family fights may produce a change in your child's speech behavior. He may repeat or hesitate more than usual. A child's speech flow is closely related to parental attitudes and family situations. Events that affect his sense of security may also affect his speech flow. Some children have a tendency to reveal their stresses in their speech. However, many children go through such stresses without their speech being affected at all.

Parents can be particularly effective in helping their children through periods of interruptions in the speech flow. Listen to *what* your child says rather than *how* he says it. In this way the child feels that what he has to say is important and that you are interested in what it is he has to say. It is best to simply ignore his speech fumblings. If *you* pay no attention to his trials and errors, neither will he. Your calm acceptance and approval of both his good and poor speech builds his self-confidence such that he can continue confidently the process of acquiring speaking skills.

Parents can unknowingly put obstacles in their children's path, and thus increase the number of repetitions or hesitations. This could be dangerous under the following circumstances. If you show concern or disapproval in your facial expression, tone of voice, or body posture when your child's speech breaks down, he, too, becomes concerned about his speech. Your child may begin to think that he is doing something wrong, that his speech is bad. For a few children, this may lay the groundwork for stuttering. Let us see how.

Assume that the child is afraid that he will make a mistake every time he opens his mouth. This fear in turn makes the child tense and subject to more interruptions in his speech than before. He feels badly about himself, and at this young age he does not have well-developed defenses to handle shame, embarrassment, and fear as well as we adults do. The act of communication may become unpleasant and fearful, and he therefore withdraws from it. Unwittingly, you may have created a situation that can lead to attitudes that produce stuttering when you cause the child to doubt his ability to talk correctly. A child is in for trouble if his effortless repetitions and sound prolongations become irregular, more numerous, and more tense. Struggling behavior then becomes evident in his speech. He is frustrated, embarrassed, and afraid to speak. Most children do, of course, develop smooth speech flow despite environmental conditions, yet parents can make this process easier for their children by following a few good habits and in turn greatly reduce the possibility of their own child developing a stuttering problem.

Parental Guidelines

What can you do to help your child during nonfluencies?

You can take some very effective steps to help your child during this period of developing smooth speech flow. These include both do's and don't's. The following is a list of do's. (1) The most important thing is to be a good listener. Pay attention to him and show him that you, too, think that what he has to say is important. Be aware of the feelings he is expressing. You may have some learning to do in order to become a good listener! (2) Listen to all of your child's speech — both the interrupted and the well-formed — with pleasure and approval. Encourage and praise his efforts, be they perfect or imperfect. He is much too young for you to demand or expect perfect speech from him. Again, if *you* pay no attention to his trials and errors, neither will he, and his speech will be spontaneous and joyful. (3) Ease the demands on your child to reply immediately. Give him a chance to formulate his thoughts. (4) You should continue to be a good speech model to your child. Speak slowly and clearly. If you always speak rapidly, he may try to speak at your rate. Your rapid rate may simply be too fast for his language ability and physical mechanism, and may cause him speech troubles. (5) Provide opportunities in which feelings can be expressed verbally. Teach your child by example how to talk about both pleasant and unpleasant feelings. Speech is a nondestructive way to blow off emotional steam. (6) Finally, be a good communication partner for your child. Take turns listening and speaking; do not let communication be a one-way street.

There are some specific things you should *not* do when your child faces confusion in thinking and talking. (1) Do not interrupt your child when he is speaking, especially when he is struggling with words. Let him take as much time as he needs to complete his thought. (2) Do not coax him to recite for others. In general, do not put him into a speaking situation which will embarrass him, should he fail to speak well. (3) Do not demand speech from your child if he is upset or crying. (4) Be especially careful not to make suggestions to him about how to talk without interruptions. For example, do not say to a child involved in speech difficulty, "Slow down," "Spit it out," "Stop and start over," or "Take a deep breath." These statements only serve to draw attention to his difficulty and to the fact that you think that something is wrong. (5) Do not discuss his speech breakdowns around him and prevent other family members from doing so. (6) Do not put too much pressure on your child to speak well in order to appear intelligent. Be familiar with developmental language patterns so that you can form *realistic* speech expectations of your child.

We have now considered some of the natural causes of the interruptions in the speech flow, and discussed some positive ways for you to react to them. We must now consider the possibility that your child is developing a speech problem. What warning signs can alert you?

1. The child begins to show marked and obvious speech hesitancies.
2. He begins to avoid verbal contact or becomes excessively shy about speaking in certain situations which he had formerly entered eagerly. The same holds true when this reluctance to speak involves a certain person.
3. He begins to speak with effort and strain, and is clearly struggling to express things which he had previously said easily.
4. Volleys of repetition of syllables or sounds, or the drawing out of sounds, begin to reappear more often (Speech Foundation of America, 1962, p. 59).

If, despite your efforts, your child seems to be developing signs of beginning to stutter, consult a speech clinician in your community as soon as possible.

Various activities stimulate your child's language development.

You and your child can have fun telling stories together at this stage. Perhaps you and your child started this at an earlier stage. If so, you probably notice an increase in his ability to tell stories. Describing pictures in books and magazines helps him make word associations. You should point out how objects are alike and how they are different. Also inform your child about why things happen; explain the reasons behind events. Playing with other children his own age will give him increased opportunity to use language. Constantly playing with older children may, however, put too much pressure on him to compete on a verbal level with them.

Physical Development

By this age your child is able to hold a pencil like an adult. He can imitate a cross and an X. He can draw his version of a man on paper, which may produce many laughs. Gross physical accomplishments include the following: (1) standing on one foot for two seconds, (2) walking down steps one foot per step. He can dress himself with a little help on fastenings and he is completely independent on the toilet. As you can see, he is becoming more skillful in his physical movements as well as his speech and language abilities.

Checkpoints

Your four-year-old child should be able to do the following:

Speech and Language Skills

(1) Talk with some natural hesitations, repetitions, and restarts.
(2) Formulate a sentence five to six words in length.
(3) Use various sentence types, such as interrogative, declarative, imperative, and negative.
(4) Understand the function of familiar objects.

(5) Use the following consonants: *p, m, h, n, w, b, k, g, d, t, -ng, f,* and *y.*
(6) Understand prepositions: *by, beside, in front of.*
(7) Use present and past tense verbs and some auxiliary verbs.
(8) Form a variety of questions.
(9) Tell a story with sequential events.

Physical Abilities

(1) Hold a pencil like an adult.
(2) Imitate a cross and an X with pencil and paper.
(3) Draw a picture of a man with several parts represented.
(4) Stand on one foot for two seconds.
(5) Walk down stairs like an adult.
(6) Be completely independent on toilet.
(7) Dress himself with help on fastenings.
(8) Brush his teeth.
(9) Pour from a pitcher.

FOUR TO FIVE YEARS
NINETY PERCENT OF THE
LANGUAGE IS LEARNED

YOUR child is nearly a full-fledged citizen of his language community. He has completed 90 percent of the job of learning speech and language skills, but not without fun and laughter, trials and tribulations. Most of his sentences are grammatically correct, or grammatically similar to adult models, as the result of a continual process of developing, discarding, and refining his language rules. The acquisition of the basic sentence types and the different parts of speech is nearly complete. However, compared with adults, his sentences are shorter and express relatively limited ideas, though they may sound adultlike. He still understands more complex language than he can formulate. His vocabulary has reached over 2200 words, but the acquisition of word meanings is not completed. He realizes that there are various meanings for one word. In general, his speech is intelligible and precise, but a few of the more complex sounds may not be perfected until six to eight years of age.

Language Development

By the age of five, differences in your grammar and that of your child are not readily apparent by simply listening. Much of what he says will be adultlike. A few difficulties remain for him to master, though. For the most part, these difficulties involve word endings. He may have trouble with subject and verb agreement, plurals, and correct usage of pronouns. The learning of the many verb tenses may not be completed. He does, however, understand the uses of *was, were, is, are* and *am.* He does not understand passive tense verbs, such as, "He *was hit* by the ball." This type of sentence violates his previously learned word order. In this case the object does something to the subject, instead of the reverse.

Your child has acquired the ability to count to ten, understand the number concepts *one, two* and *three,* can name coins, and use all question words. If you give him four consecutive simple commands he should be able to execute them, for example: "Put the ball under the chair, bring me the pencil, close the door, and come here." He understands almost everything you say, even in its complicated adult form.

Language now begins to take on new functions for your child. That is, language begins to play an important role in his ability to remember. The accuracy with which he remembers an event depends on how well he coded the experience into words. If he wants to remember something, he converts it into language. Suppose he is shown three pictures. If he repeats the names of the pictures to himself, he has a better chance of telling you what the three pictures were later. He stores the names, not the visual images of the pictures. In a year he will perfect this skill. We adults do the same thing without even realizing it. In this way we remember events, objects, and phone numbers. We use language for self-guidance in undertaking a task. For example, we think to ourselves, "... first I need to go to the store, then the bank, and finally the laundry." Your child is acquiring this skill, also — to use the language for self-guidance.

Your child makes use of several types of language.

The preschool child is only aware of his own point of view of the world around him. He does not understand that there are other points of view than his own. However, around six years of age he does begin to change in this respect. His inability to understand other points of view affects his communicative ability in that he fails to understand the role of his listener. Therefore, he seldom meets the information needs of the listener and his listeners are not able to completely understand the child's message. This situation produces what is called "egocentric" speech as opposed to "socialized" speech. Egocentric speech is that speech used when alone, or in the presence of others, that lacks clear communicative intent. It resembles a monologue the child carries on out loud with himself. All preschool children exhibit egocentric speech at some time. In fact, 45 percent of preschooler's utterances are of this nature. This behavior decreases until, at about the age of six, it is replaced by socialized speech. Socialized speech is directed at a listener for some purpose. It is the child's commands, answers, questions, and comments. It has a definite communication purpose, and the child relates something in sufficient detail to be understood.

Speech Development

How good is your child's pronunciation?

During the various stages, your child acquired new, increasingly more complex sounds. To his repertoire he now adds the *th-* sound. His speech will be clear and intelligible to adults, but words containing the following sounds may not yet be pronounced correctly: *r, s, l, ch-, sh-, z, v, th-,* or *j.* These are the sounds that he will be practicing, and perhaps not saying perfectly until eight years of age. Consonant clusters (*str, bl, sp*) may yet be difficult for him to say, as well. Each child differs in his rate of sound acquisition, and various factors in the child's environment may affect this rate in one way or another. Such things as physical handicaps, illness, hearing impairment, lack of good speech models, lack of speech stimulation, or many other children in the family may act to slow the rate of acquisition of speech sounds.

Parental Guidelines

Where do you find help for speech problems?

If you think that your child may have a speech and/or language problem, the earlier you refer him to a speech clinician, the greater are his chances of improvement. With a firm understanding of speech and language processes, you are better able to decide whether or not your child needs to be referred to a specialist.

Speech and language services may be found in the following locations: (1) university clinics, (2) clinics run by the Easter Seal Society for Crippled Children and Adults, (3) public schools and kindergartens, (4) Head Start Programs, (5) rehabilitation centers for crippled children and adults, and (6) facilities offering private practice. If you know of no such institutions or centers near you, contact your state department of education or the American Speech and Hearing Association. They will provide you with information concerning the location of the speech and language services nearest you. The address of the American Speech and Hearing Association is 9030 Old Georgetown Road, Washington, D. C., 20014.

Physical Development

Your child's physical development is not completed.

A child of this age should be able to dress and undress himself (except for tying his shoes). He can jump rope, skip, and balance on one foot for ten seconds. With his hands he can color a simple picture, cut with scissors, copy a square and a triangle, and draw a man with the body parts in the correct places. His language skills are nearly complete, but he has a long way to go before he acquires 90 percent of his physical abilities.

Checkpoints

You should be concerned if you observe any of the following (Staff of Developmental Language and Speech Center, 1970, pp. 105-6):

Speech and Language Skills

(1) Your child does not appear to respond to sounds in his

environment by six months of age.

(2) Your child is not talking at all by the age of two years.

(3) His speech is largely unintelligible after the age of three.

(4) He is leaving off many beginning consonants after the age of three.

(5) He is still not using two to three-word sentences by the age of three.

(6) Sounds are more than a year late in appearing in his speech according to their developmental sequence (see Table I).

(7) He uses mostly vowel sounds in his speech after one year of age.

(8) His word endings are consistently missing after the age of five.

(9) His sentence structure is noticeably faulty at the age of five.

(10) He is embarrassed and disturbed by his speech at any age.

(11) He is noticeably producing interruptions in his speech after the age of six.

(12) He is making speech errors after the age of eight.

(13) His voice is a monotone, too loud or too soft, or of a poor quality that may indicate a hearing loss.

(14) His voice quality is too high or too low for his age and sex.

(15) He sounds as if he were talking through his nose, or as if he has a cold.

(16) His speech has abnormal rhythm, rate, and inflection after the age of five.

GLOSSARY

Auxiliary Verb. A helping verb that joins with the main verb to form a different tense, mood, or voice. Examples: *have, has, may, can, do, will.*

Babbling. As used here, the child's vocalizations from his earliest coos and gurgles up to, but not including, his first words. The child begins to babble at about six to seven weeks of age.

Cognitive Development. The development of the child's thinking ability. The acquisition of information or knowledge for reasoning and understanding by observing the environment and drawing conclusions about it.

Concepts. A general idea, understanding, or conclusion about the environment. For example, a child forms the concept that objects fall downward if dropped, not upward. The child also forms concepts of time. number, space, size, shape, etc.

Consonant Cluster. A consonant in a word in combination with one or more other consonants. Examples: *str-, bl-, spl-.* Each consonant is pronounced.

Consonant Positions. Traditionally, sounds have been located in the initial, medial, and final positions in words. The initial position is at the beginning of a word. The medial position is any consonant in a word that does not begin or end it. The final position is the consonant at the end of the word.

Egocentric Speech. Self-oriented speech in which the child vocalizes his own perceptual processes, things he has seen, felt, or heard. Children at this stage in language development are unable to see the world from another's point of view. For example, the child cannot understand and therefore does not talk about how his mother's sore finger hurts.

Expressive Language. Language that is formulated and coded into our speech sounds in the form of words and sentences.

Grammar. The system of rules implicit in a language. We use grammar to construct our sentences and utterances and judge whether language is in a correct or incorrect form.

Hearing Impairment. The partial loss of the ability to hear, whether severe or slight.

Inflection. The changes in pitch of our voice during an utterance, used as an element of meaning in the language to express surprise, ask a question, or to emphasize.

Innate. The information or abilities that a child is born with; that which he

79

does not have to learn, assuming the usual environmental support.

Jargon. The child's continuous, unintelligible babbling, which, because of the use of inflection, resembles sentences. It usually begins around eight months of age and disappears around two years of age.

Language. The complex symbol system or code which we use to express ideas, thoughts, and messages to others, in vocal or written form.

Language Scheme. The language system that any individual, child or adult, has developed through the formulation of a set of rules of grammar. A child's language scheme constantly increases in complexity.

Maturational Process. Those processes of mental, physical, and behavioral growth by which the child attains full development. Growth in the neurological and muscular systems of the child allow kinds of behavior and thinking which were not possible earlier.

Nonlinguistic Experience. The exploration and information gathering that a child does by seeing, feeling, smelling, tasting, and hearing things around him. This information enables him to form concepts which are vitally important for language development.

Nonverbal Communication. That form of communicating with others that does not involve speech or language, but rather facial expressions, body postures, gestures, and physical contact.

Noun Phrase. A group of words containing a noun and all of its modifiers or adjectives, such as "the big old *hat*," or "that red *flower* with the green leaves."

Number Concept. The understanding of numbers in the collective sense; that is, the understanding of the magnitude of numbers. Significant development must take place before children are able to recognize groups of objects. For example, the child who understands the number concept of *three* can give you three marbles on request or can match an array of three marbles.

Parts of Speech. Members of word classes performing a specific function in a sentence. They are the different parts of a sentence, such as nouns, verbs, prepositions, adjectives, pronouns, conjunctions, articles, verbs, etc.

Perception. The act of gathering and organizing information through the senses of seeing, feeling, hearing, tasting, and smelling. Perception is a basic component in the formation of concepts.

Receptive Language. Language we hear from a speaker and interpret.

Repetitions. The repeating of the same speech sound, syllable, or word over and over again in the speech flow.

Rule Governed. That which is dictated and directed by specific rules. Normal language behavior is rule governed.

Socialized Speech. Speech revealing an awareness of the listener's feelings, concerns, and knowledge. It is directed at a listener in such a way as to be understood. This type of speech is characteristic of any one over six years of age.

Sound Boundary. The limits of the variation in mouth, tongue positions, air pressure, voicing, etc., which are used in the production of a particular speech sound. These aspects of production of a particular sound may vary somewhat, and still produce a recognizable version of the sound.

Sound Distortion. A speech sound that is pronounced with a slight variation from the standard adult sound. The resulting sound is one not normally used in English. Some, but not all of the characteristics of the sound have been changed.

Sound Omission. An error occurring in a word in which a speech sound is entirely omitted, for example "poon" for *spoon*, "lat" for *last*.

Sound Substitution. An error in a word pronunciation made by substituting a sound which can be produced for one that cannot be produced, for example, *d*at for *th*at, *w*ed for *r*ed, or *w*ittle for *l*ittle.

Sound System. The rules and speech sounds that an individual uses to produce words. The child's sound system in the beginning is not exactly like that of the adult. Over time his sound system more closely approximates that of the adult, as he acquires the adult speech sounds and the rules for using those sounds.

Speech. The coordination of muscles and airflow that is required to communicate through conventional vocal and oral symbols.

Speech Flow. The syllables of a sentence patterned in time to produce a rhythm characteristic of English. Changes in the speaker's pitch and stress contribute to this rhythm.

Speech Sounds. All the different sounds that make up English words. Each speech sound is made up of its own particular characteristics by which it is recognized as different from all of the other sounds.

Startle Response. A sudden, generalized body movement or cessation of body movement in the infant; such responses are evoked by the presentation of a loud sound. A startle response is typical of an infant's reaction to sound up to about three months of age.

Storage and Formulation Space. The language centers of the brain. The capacity of language centers to handle complex language increases as the child develops. Among the kinds of language knowledge stored are words and grammatical rules.

Telegraphic Speech. Speech — typical of the young child — that retains those words he knows how to use and which are most meaningful to him. For example, he may say, "Car broken down," rather than, "The car has broken down," omitting the auxiliary verb and the article.

Utterance. A string of words or nonmeaningful syllables uttered in one breath.

Verb Phrase. A phrase made up of a verb and its modifiers or objects. It lacks a subject. Examples are *ride* in a car, *placed* car on table, *saw* the car, *play* with the wagon.

Vocalization. Any sounds that the child produces with his voice, including cries, coos, gurgles, speech sounds, or words.

Vocal Play. The baby's voicing of sequences of sounds or syllables over and over again for enjoyment and experimentation. A three to four-month-old baby begins this more sophisticated babbling. For example, he says, "ma-ma-ma-ma," or "de-da-do-dum."

Word Class. A group of different words that may have the same function or purpose in a sentence. Examples of adult word classes are nouns, verbs, adjectives, etc.

BIBLIOGRAPHY

Berry, M.: *Language Disorders in Children: The Bases and Diagnosis*. New York, Appleton, 1969.

Berry, M., and Eisenson, J.: *Speech Disorders*. New York, Appleton, 1956.

Bloom, L.: Why not pivotal grammar? *J Speech Hear Disord, 33*:40-50, 1971.

Bloom, L.: *Form and Function in Emerging Grammars*. Cambridge, M.I.T. Pr, 1970.

Boone, D. R.: *The Voice and Voice Therapy*. Englewood Cliffs, P-H, 1971.

Bowlby, J.: *Attachment and Loss, Volume I*. New York, Basic, 1969.

Branscom, M., Hughes, J., and Oxtoby, E.: Studies of nonfluency in speech of preschool children. In Johnson, W. (Ed.): *Stuttering in Children and Adults*. Minneapolis, U of Minn Pr, 1955.

Broen, P. A.: *The Verbal Environment of the Language Learning Child*. American Speech and Hearing Association Monograph. Number 17, 1972.

Brown, R.: *A First Language*. Cambridge, Harvard U Pr, 1973.

Brown, R.: How shall a thing be called? In Dale, P.: *Language Development — Structure and Function*. Hinsdale, Dryden, 1972.

Brown, R.: *Psycholinguistics*. New York, Free Pr, 1970.

Brown, R., and Bellugi, U. (Eds.): *The Acquisition of Language*. Society for Research in Child Development Monograph, 29, 1, 1964.

Brown, R., and Bellugi, U.: Three processes in the child's acquisition of syntax. *Harvard Education Review, 34*:133-151, 1964.

Brown, R., and Hanlon, C.: Derivational complexity and order of acquisition in child speech. In Hayes, J. (Ed.): *Cognition and the Development of Language*. New York, Wiley, 1970.

Bzoch, K., and League, R.: *Assessing Skills in Infancy*. Gainesville, Tree of Life Pr, 1971.

Carrow, M. A.: The development of auditory comprehension of language structure in children. *J Speech Hear Disord, 33*:105-108, 1968.

Carrow, M. A.: Language disorders: A theory. In Harry Jersig Speech and Hearing Center (Ed.): *A Theoretical Approach to Diagnosis and Treatment of Language Disorders in Children*. San Antonio, Our Lady of the Lake College, 1968.

Cazden, C.: *Child Language and Education*. New York, HR&W, 1972.

Clark, E.: Some aspects of the conceptual basis of the first language. In Schiefelbusch, R., and Lloyd, L. (Eds): *Language Perspectives — Acquisition, Retardation, and Intervention*, Baltimore, University Park

Pr, 1974.

Clark, E.: On the child's acquisition of semantics in his first language. In Moore, T. (Ed.): *Cognitive Development and the Acquisition of Language.* New York, Acad Pr, 1973.

Clements, S., Davis, J., Goolsby, D., and Peters, J.: *Physician's Handbook, Screening for Minimal Brain Dysfunction.* Summit, Ciba Med Horizons, 1973.

Compton, A.: Generative Studies of Children's Phonological Disorders. *J Speech Hear Disord, 35:*315-340, 1970

Cratty, B. J.: *Perceptual and Motor Development in Infants and Children.* London, Macmillan, 1970.

Crocker, J.: A phonological model of children's articulation competence. *J Speech Hear Disord, 34:*203-212, 1969.

Cruttenden, A.: A phonetic study of babbling. *Br J Disord Commun, 5:*110-117, 1970.

Dale, P. S.: *Language Development — Structure and Function.* Hinsdale, Dryden, 1972.

Dene, P. D., and Pinson, E. N.: *The Speech Chain.* Bell Telephone Laboratories, 1963.

Downs, M. P., and Northern, J. L.: *Hearing in Children.* Baltimore, Williams & Wilkins, 1974.

Easter Seal Society for Crippled Children and Adults: *Helping Your Child Learn to Talk — Suggestions for Parents.* Sacramento, Easter Seal Society, n.d.

Egland, G.: Repetitions and prolongations in the speech of stuttering and nonstuttering children. In Johnson, W. (Ed.): *Stuttering in Children and Adults.* Minneapolis, U Minn Pr, 1955.

Ervin-Tripp, S.: How children answer questions. In Hayes, J. (Ed.): *Cognition and the Development of Language.* New York, Wiley, 1970.

Erwin, R. B.: *A Speech Pathologist Talks to Parents and Teachers.* Pittsburgh, Stanwix, 1962.

Friedlander, B. Z.: Receptive language development in infancy. *Merrill-Palmer Quarterly, 16:*7-51, 1970.

Ginsburg, H., and Opper, S.: *Piaget's Theory of Intellectual Development — An Introduction.* Englewood Cliffs, P-H, 1969.

Hayes, C.: *The Ape in Our House.* New York, Har-Row, 1951.

Hayes, J. (Ed.): *Cognition and the Development of Language.* New York, Wiley, 1970.

Hodgson, W. R.: Testing infants and young children. In Katz, J. (Ed.): *Handbook of Clinical Audiology.* Baltimore, Williams & Wilkins, 1972.

Hopper, R., and Naremore, R.: *Children's Speech: A Practical Introduction to Communication Development.* New York, Har-Row, 1973.

Irwin, O. C.: Infant speech: the development of vowel sounds. *J Speech Disord, 13:*31-34, 1948.

Irwin, O. C.: Infant speech: consonant sounds according to place of articulation. *J Speech Disord, 12:*397-401, 1947.

Jesperson, O.: *Language.* New York, HR&W, 1925.

Jones, M.: *Baby Talk.* Springfield, Thomas, 1960.

Jones, M.: *Speech Correction at Home.* Springfield, Thomas, 1957.

Katz, J., and Struckman, S.: A case history of children. In Katz, J. (Ed.): *Handbook of Clinical Audiology.* Baltimore, Williams & Wilkins, 1972.

Knauf, V. H.: Meeting speech and language needs for the hearing impaired. In Katz, J. (Ed.): *Handbook of Clinical Audiology.* Baltimore, Williams & Wilkins, 1972.

Landreth, C.: *Early Childhood: Behavior and Learning.* New York, Knopf, 1967.

Lassers, L.: *Eight Keys to Normal Speech and Child Development.* State Department of Education, Oregon, 1945.

Lee, L., and Canter, S.: Developmental sentence scoring: a clinical procedure for estimating syntactical development in children's spontaneous speech. *J Speech Hear Disord, 36:*317-340, 1971.

Lee, L.: Developmental sentence types: a method for comparing normal and deviant syntactical development. *J Speech Hear Disord, 31:*311-330, 1966.

Lenneberg, E.: *Biological Foundations of Language.* New York, Wiley, 1967.

Lieberman, P.: *Intonation, Perception, and Language.* Cambridge, M.I.T. Pr, 1967.

Locke, J.: Ease of articulation. *J Speech Hear Disord, 15:*194-200, 1972.

Long, C.: *Will Your Child Learn to Talk Correctly?* Albuquerque, N Mexico Pub, 1957.

McCarthy, D.: Language development in children. In Carmichael, L. (Ed.): *Manual of Child Psychology.* New York, Wiley, 1954

McClean, M. E.: Introduction: developing clinical strategies for language intervention with mentally retarded children. In McClean, J., Yoder, D., and Schiefelbusch, R. (Eds.): *Language Intervention with the Retarded.* Baltimore, University Park Pr, 1972.

McNeill, D.: *The Acquisition of Language — The Study of Developmental Psycholinguistics.* New York, Har-Row, 1970.

McNeill, D.: Developmental psycholinguistics. In Smith, F., and Miller, A. (Eds.): *The Genesis of Language.* Cambridge, M.I.T. Pr, 1966.

McReynolds, L. V., and Houston, K.: A distinctive feature analysis of children's misarticulations. *J Speech Hear Disord, 36:*155-166, 1971.

Marler, P.: Birdsong and speech development: could there be parallels? *Am Sci, 58:*669-673, 1970.

Mecham, M.: *Verbal Language Development Scale.* Minneapolis, American Guidance Service, Inc., 1959.

Menyuk, P.: Early development of receptive language: from babbling to words. In Schiefelbush, R., and Lloyd, L. (Eds.): *Language*

Perspectives — Acquisition, Retardation, and Intervention. Baltimore, University Park Pr, 1974.

Menyuk, P.: *The Development of Speech.* New York, Bobbs, 1972.

Menyuk, P.: *Sentences Children Use.* Cambridge, M.I.T. Pr, 1969.

Menyuk, P.: The role of distinctive features in children's acquisition of phonology. *J Speech Hear Res, 11*:138-146, 1968.

Metraux, R.: Speech profiles of the preschool child — 18 to 54 months. *J Speech Hear Disord, 15*:37-53, 1950.

Miller, W., and Ervin, S.: The development of grammar in child language. In Bellugi, U., and Brown, R. (Eds.): *The Acquisition of Language.* Society for Research in Child Development Monograph, 29, 1, 1964.

Morehead, D., and Morehead, A.: Piagetian view of thought and language during the first two years. In Schiefelbusch, R., and Lloyd, L. (Eds.): *Language Perspectives — Acquisition, Retardation, and Intervention.* Baltimore, University Park Pr, 1974.

Moyers, R.: Postnatal development of orofacial musculature. In *Patterns of Orofacial Growth and Development.* American Speech and Hearing Association Proceedings of the Conference, Ann Arbor, Michigan, 1970.

Muma, J.: Language intervention: two questions and ten techniques. *Language, Speech, and Hearing Service in Schools,* Number 5. American Speech and Hearing Association, 1971.

Mysak, E. D.: Cerebral palsy speech syndromes. *Handbook of Speech Pathology and Audiology.* New York, Appleton, 1971.

National Institute of Neurological Disease and Stroke: *Learning to Talk — Speech, Hearing, and Language Problems in the Preschool Child.* Bethesda, National Institute of Neurological Disease and Stroke, 1969.

Palmer, C.: *Speech and Hearing Problems — A Guide for Parents and Teachers.* Springfield, Thomas, 1961.

Perkell, J. A.: *Physiology of Speech Production.* Cambridge, M.I.T. Pr, 1969.

Power, M. H.: Functional disorders of articulation — symptomatology and egiology. In Travis, L. (Ed.): *Handbook of Speech Pathology and Audiology.* New York, Appleton, 1971.

Prather, E., Hedrick, D., and Kern, C.: Articulation development in children. *J Speech Hear Disord 40*:174-191, 1975.

Routh, D.: Conditioning of vocal response differentiation in infants. *Dev Psychol, 1*:219-226, 1969.

Sanders, D. A.: Visual and auditory rehabilitation for children. In Katz, J. (Ed.): *Handbook of Clinical Audiology.* Baltimore, Williams & Wilkins, 1972.

Sanders, E.: When are speech sounds learned? *J Speech Hear Disord, 37*:55-63, 1972.

Sanders, E.: How significant is a baby's babbling? *Elementary English, 46*:80-84, 1969.

Sayre, J.: *Helping the Child to Listen and Talk.* Danville, Interstate, 1966.

Schiefelbusch, R., and Lloyd, L. (Eds.): *Language Perspectives —
Acquisition, Retardation, and Intervention.* Baltimore, University Park
Pr, 1974.

Sklar, M.: *How Children Learn to Speak.* Los Angeles, Western Psych, 1969.

Snow, K.: Analysis of "normal" articulation responses. *J Speech Hear Res,
6*:279-290, 1963.

Slobin, D. (Ed.): *The Ontogenesis of Grammar — A Theoretical Symposium.*
New York, Acad Pr, 1971a.

Slobin, D.: *Psycholinguistics.* Greenview, Scott F, 1971b.

Slobin, D.: Universals of grammatic development in children. In Flores
d'Arcais, G., and Levelt, W. (Eds.): *Advances in Psycholinguistics.*
Amsterdam, North Holland, 1970.

Speech Foundation of America: *Stuttering: Its Prevention.* Memphis, Speech
Foundation of America, 1962.

Spock, B.: *Baby and Child Care.* New York, Cardinal, 1957.

Staff of Developmental Language and Speech Center: *Teach Your Child To
Talk — A Parent Handbook.* Grand Rapids, Cebco Standard Pub,
1970.

Sweeney, S.: The importance of imitation in the early stages of speech
acquisition. *J Speech Hear Disord, 39*:490-494, 1973.

Templin, M.: Speech development in the young child: the development of
certain language skills in children. *J Speech Hear Disord, 17*:280-285,
1962.

U. S. Department of Health, Education, and Welfare, Children's Bureau:
Your Child From 1 To 3. Washington, D. C., U. S. Government
Printing Office, 1973.

U. S. Department of Health, Education, and Welfare, Children's Bureau:
Your Child From 1 To 6. Washington, D. C., U. S. Government
Printing Office, 1962.

Van Riper, C.: *Speech Correction — Principles and Practices.* Englewood
Cliffs, P-H, 1972.

Van Riper, C.: *Helping Children Talk Better.* Chicago, Sci Research Assoc,
1951.

Van Riper, C.: *Teaching Your Child to Talk.* New York, Har-Row, 1950.

Weeks, T.: Speech registers in young children. *Child Dev, 42*:1119-1131, 1971.

Winitz, H.: *Articulatory Acquisition and Behavior.* New York, Har-Row,
1969.

Winitz, H.: Repetitions in the vocalizations and speech of children in the first
two years of life. In *Studies of Speech Disfluency and Rate of Stutterers
and Nonstutterers.* Journal of Speech and Hearing Disorders
Monograph Number 7, 1961.

Wyatt, G.: *Language and Communication Disorders in Children.* New York,
Free Pr, 1969.

INDEX

B

Babbling (*see also* Speech sounds, early practice)

C

Checkpoints
  interpretation of, 14
  purpose of, vii
Communication
  definition of, 3
  early failure, studies of, 5
  early nonverbal, 5-6
Concepts, formation of, 6-7
Consonants (*see also* Speech sounds)
  clusters, 75
  difficult to make, 65
  easy to make, 26-27
  first used, 18
  used 18-24 months, 39, 42
  used 2-3 years, 48, 54-55
  used 3-4 years, 65, 71
  used 4-5 years, 75
Crying
  differentiation, 10-11
  importance of, 11

E

Environment, for language learning, noisy, 7
Experience, nonlinguistic, 4-7, 20, 64

G

Gestures
  importance of, 10, 13-14
  parents use of, 20
Grammar
  adult-like, 73-74
  complexity of, 57-58
  definition of, 33
  early beginnings of, 33-34
  how children learn it, 34, 44-45
  rules learned, 59

H

Hearing impairment, 21

I

Imitation
  first beginnings of, 19-20, 22, 30
  in language learning, 40

J

Jargon
  definition of, 19
  occurrence of, 19, 23

L

Language
  acquisition of, first born, 8
  egocentric, 74-75
  role in remembering, 74
  socialized, 75
  teaching techniques, 51-52
Language, expressive (*see also* Words, first and Word Combinations)
  definition of, 3
  typical 12-18 months, 23-24
  typical 18-24 months, 35-38
  typical 2-3 years, 43-45
  typical 3-4 years, 59
  typical 4-5 years, 73-75
Language, receptive

89

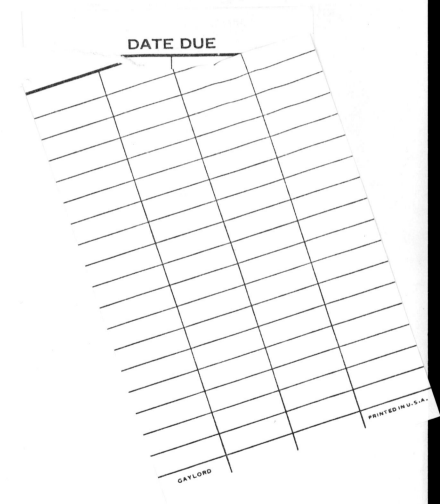

DATE DUE

GAYLORD

PRINTED IN U.S.A.